Egypt Every Day

Yasser Alwan

For Ali

Egypt Every Day

Yasser Alwan

With an essay by
Shamoon Zamir

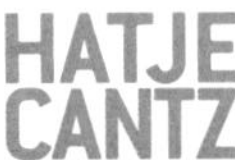

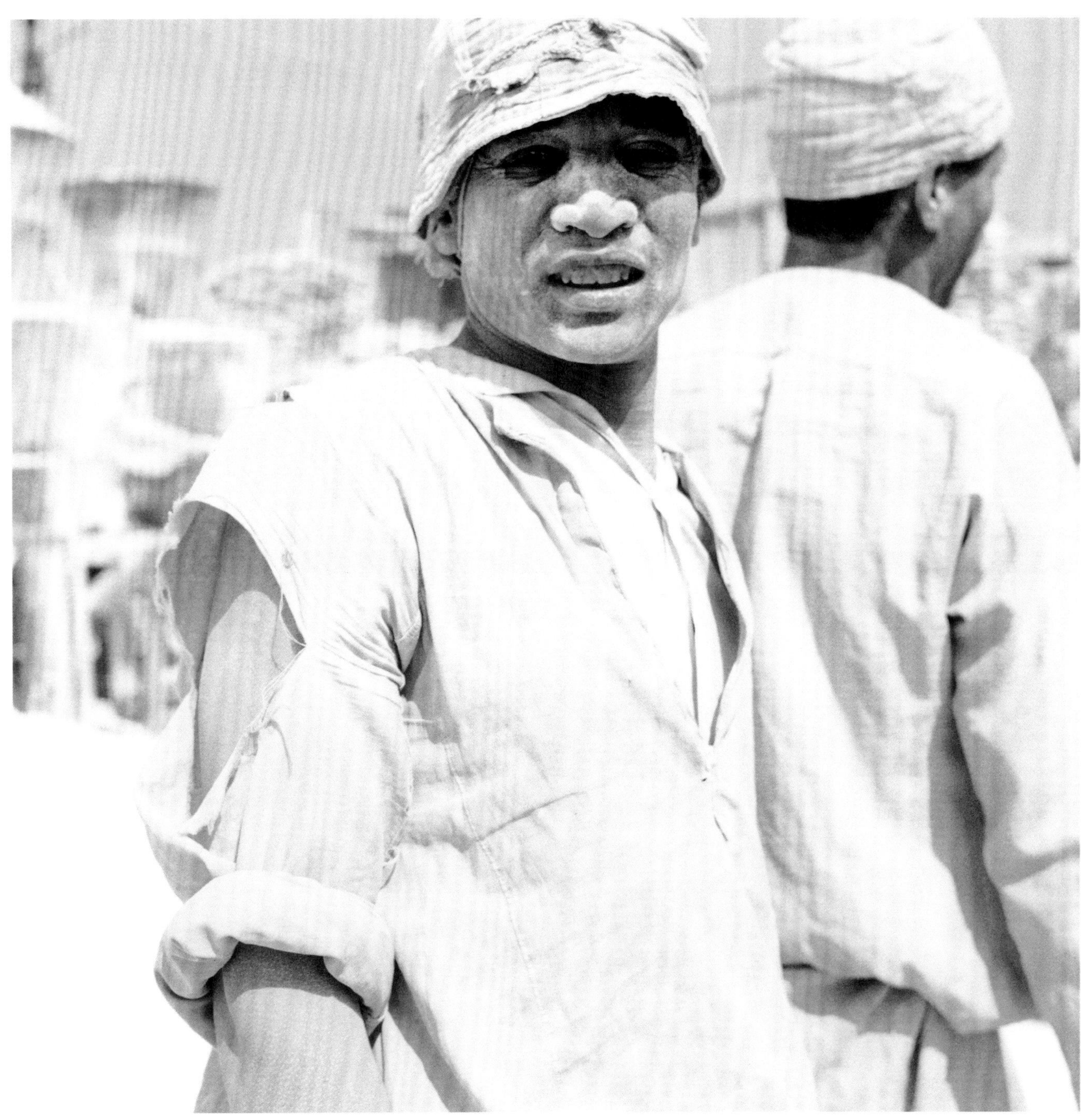

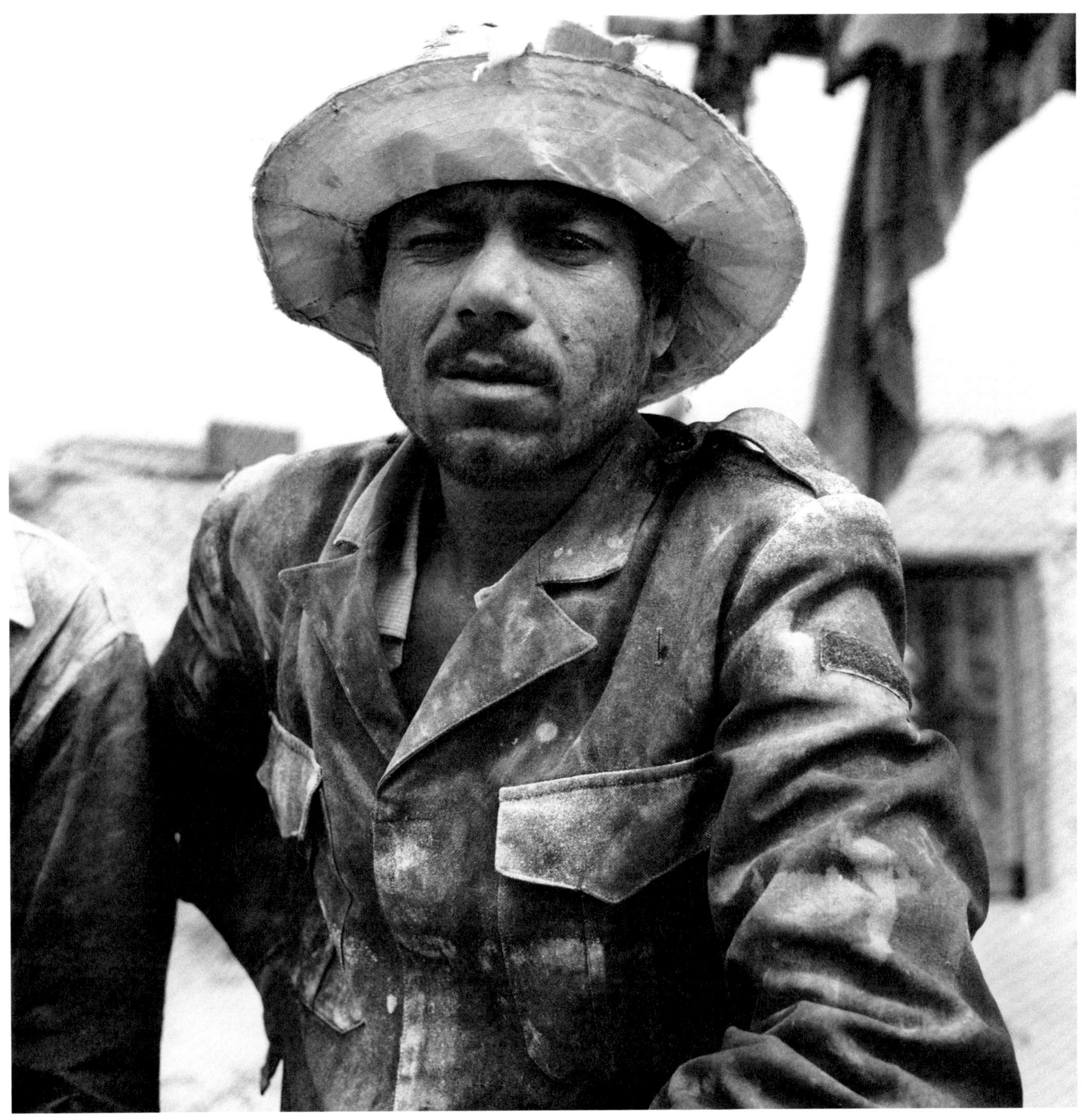

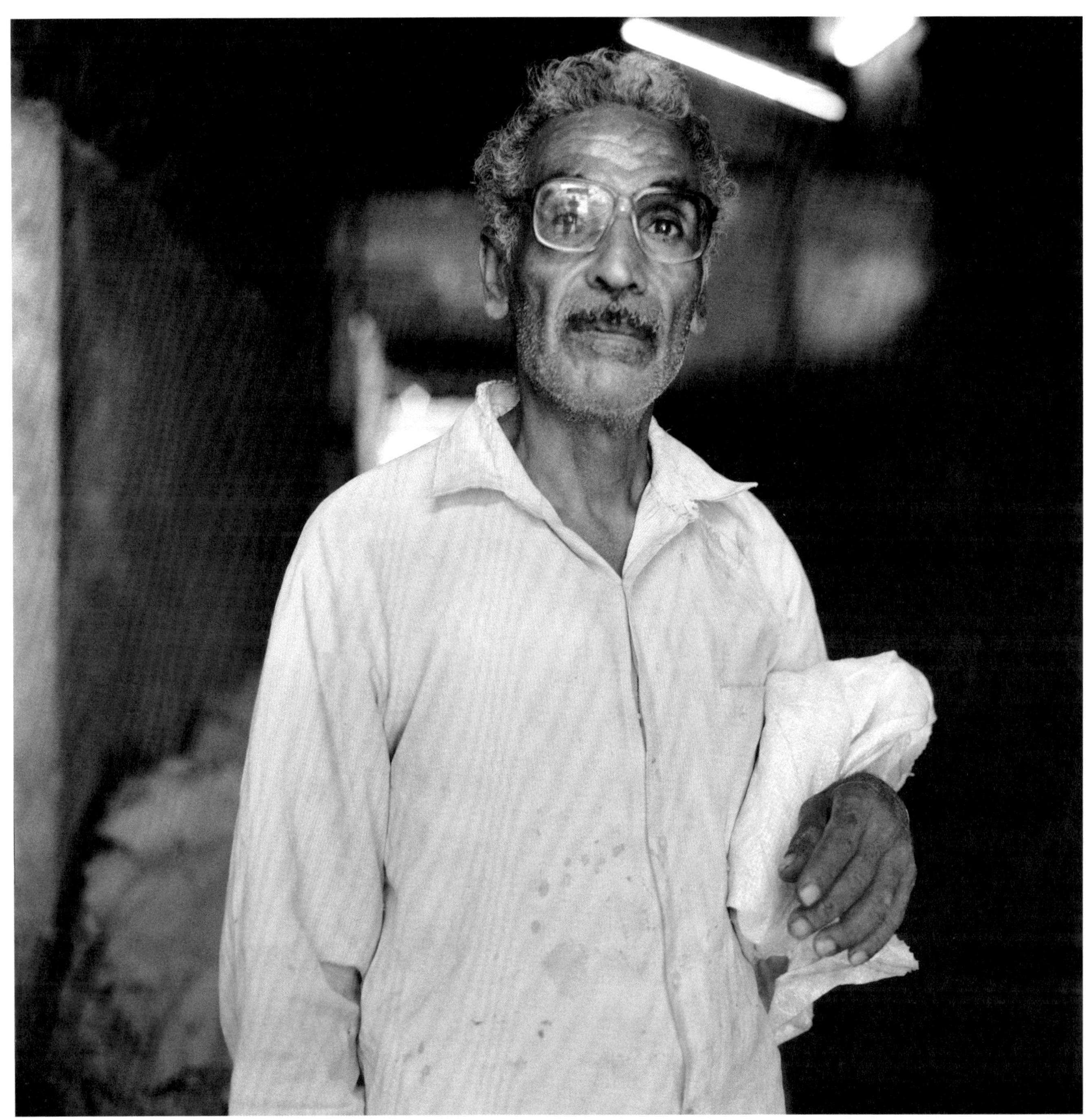

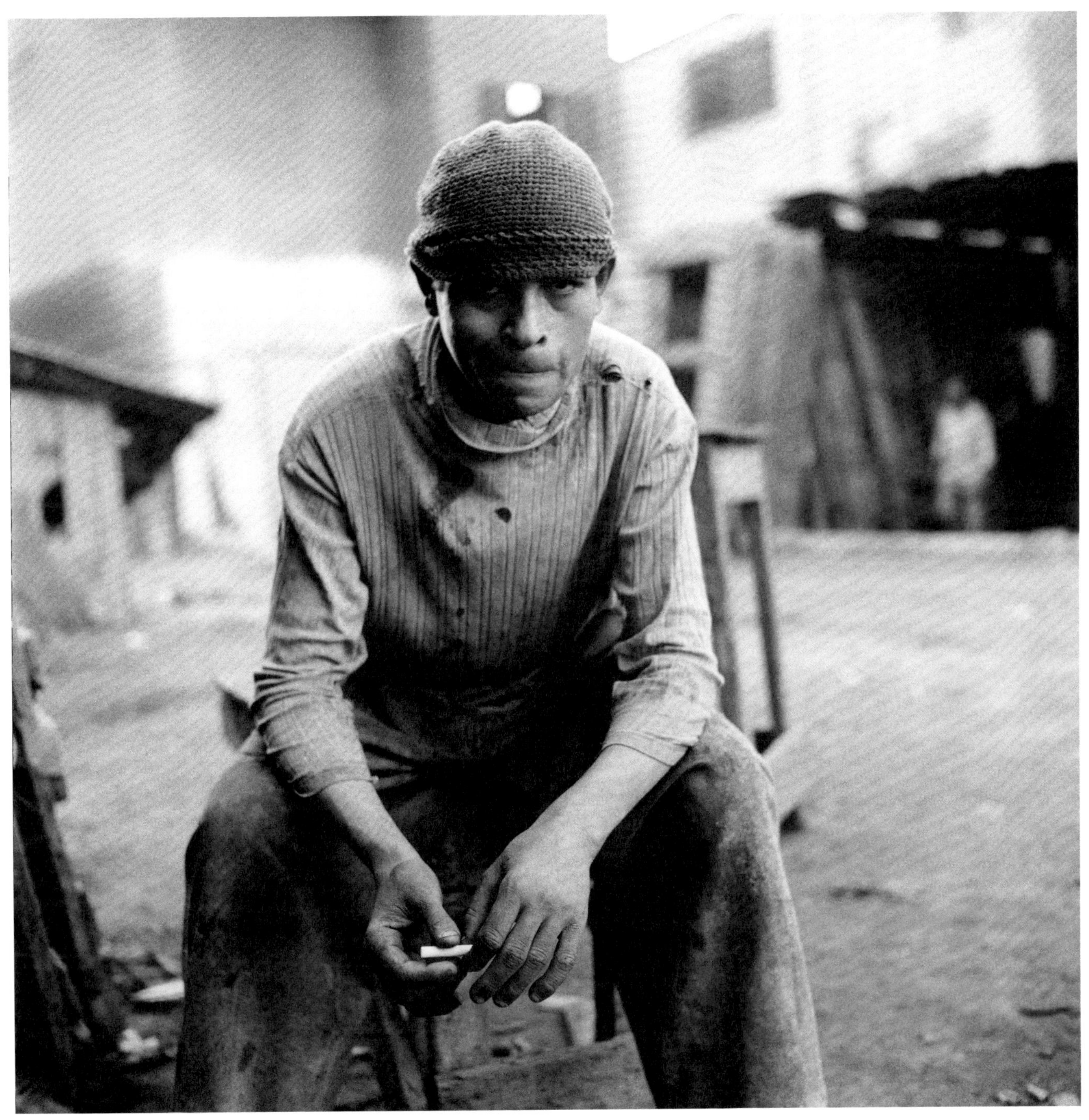

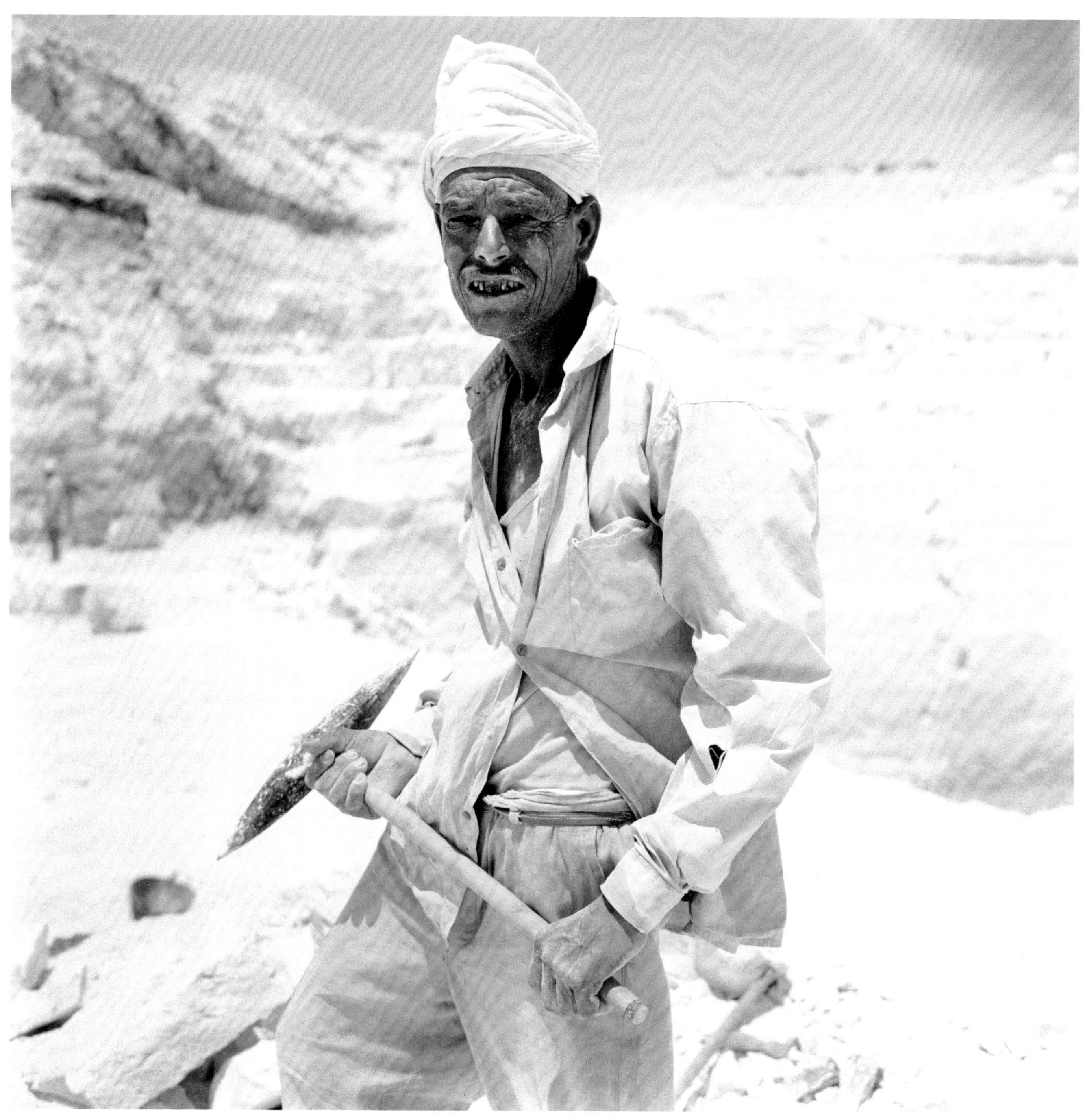

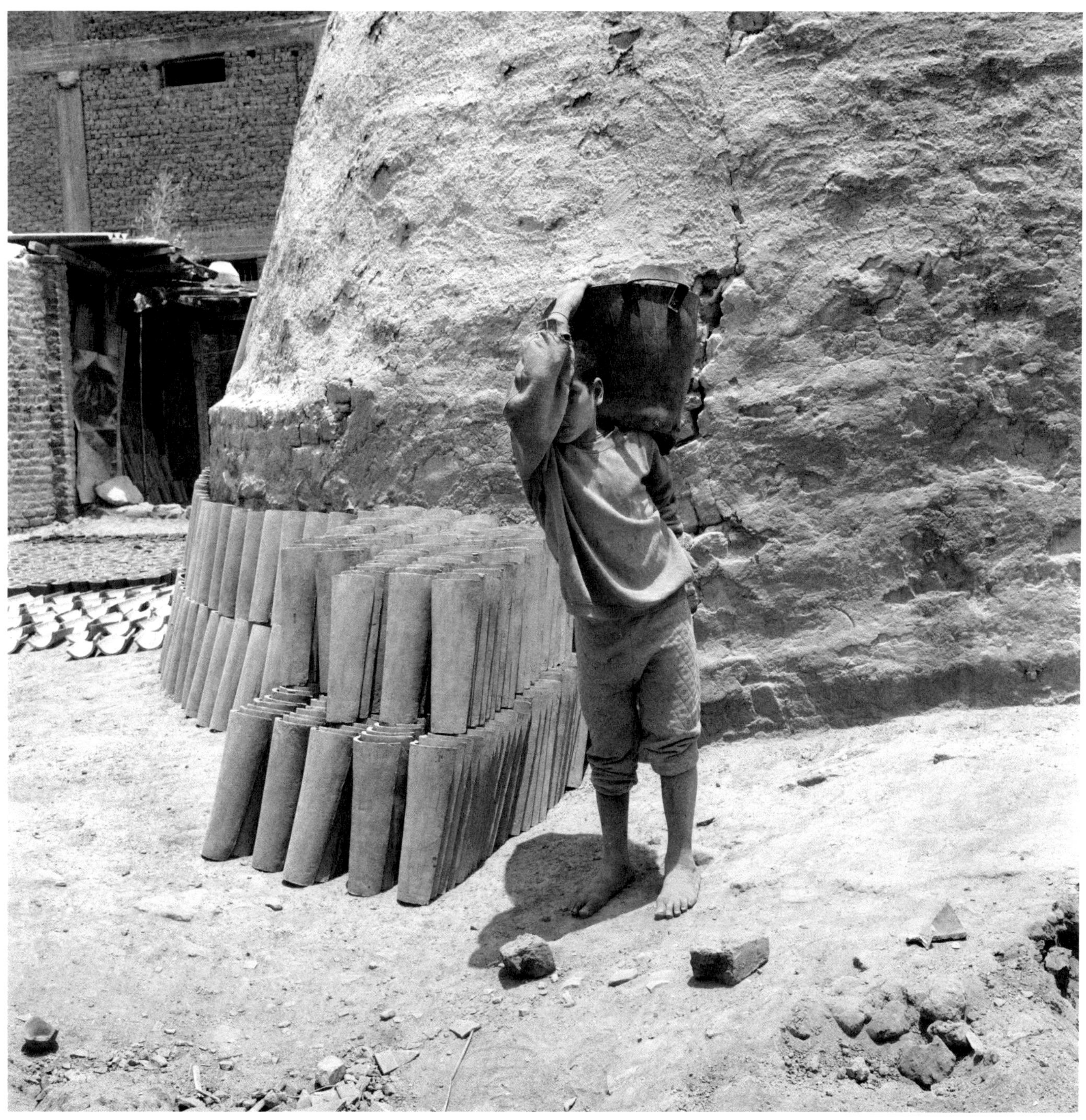

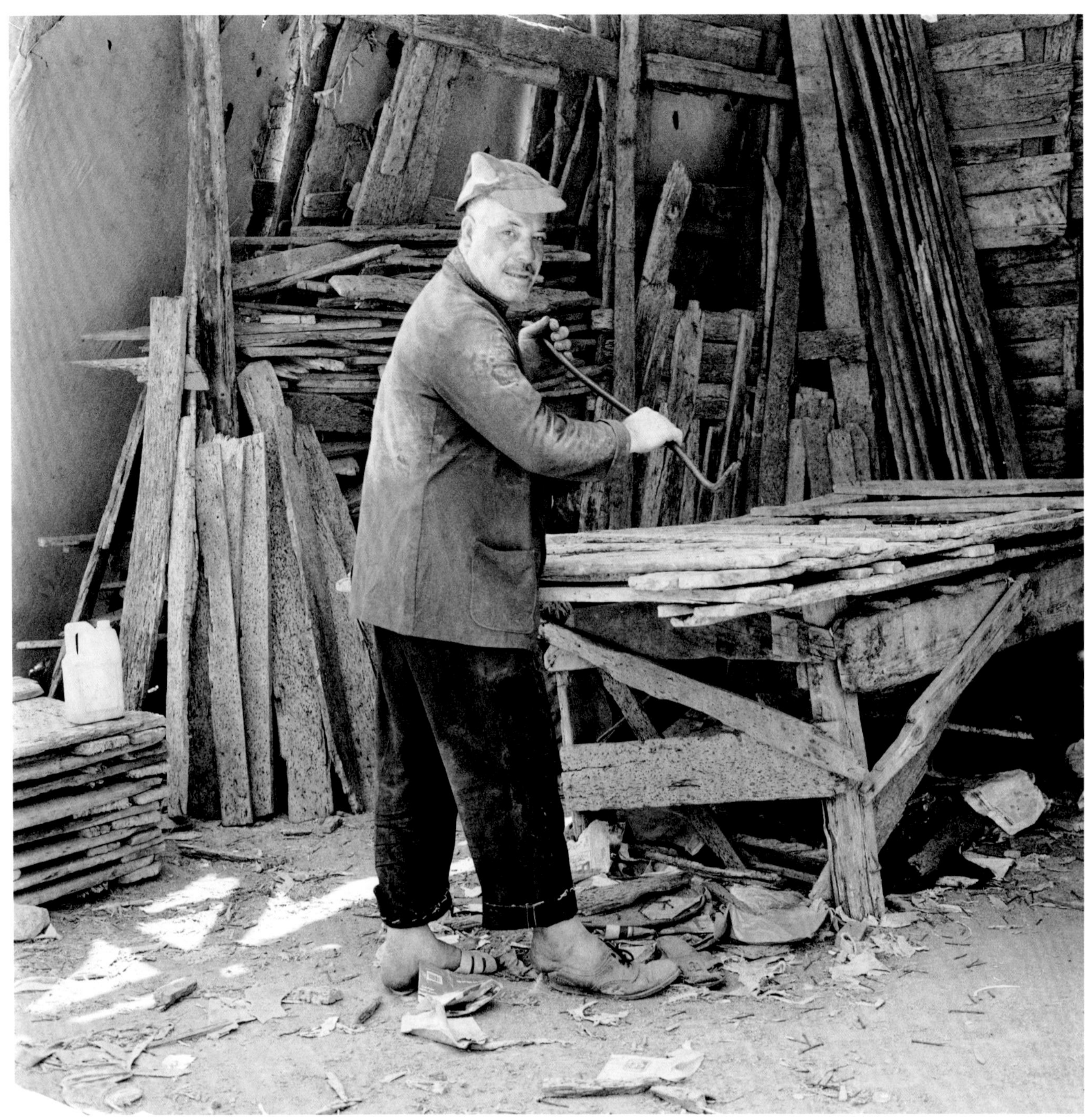

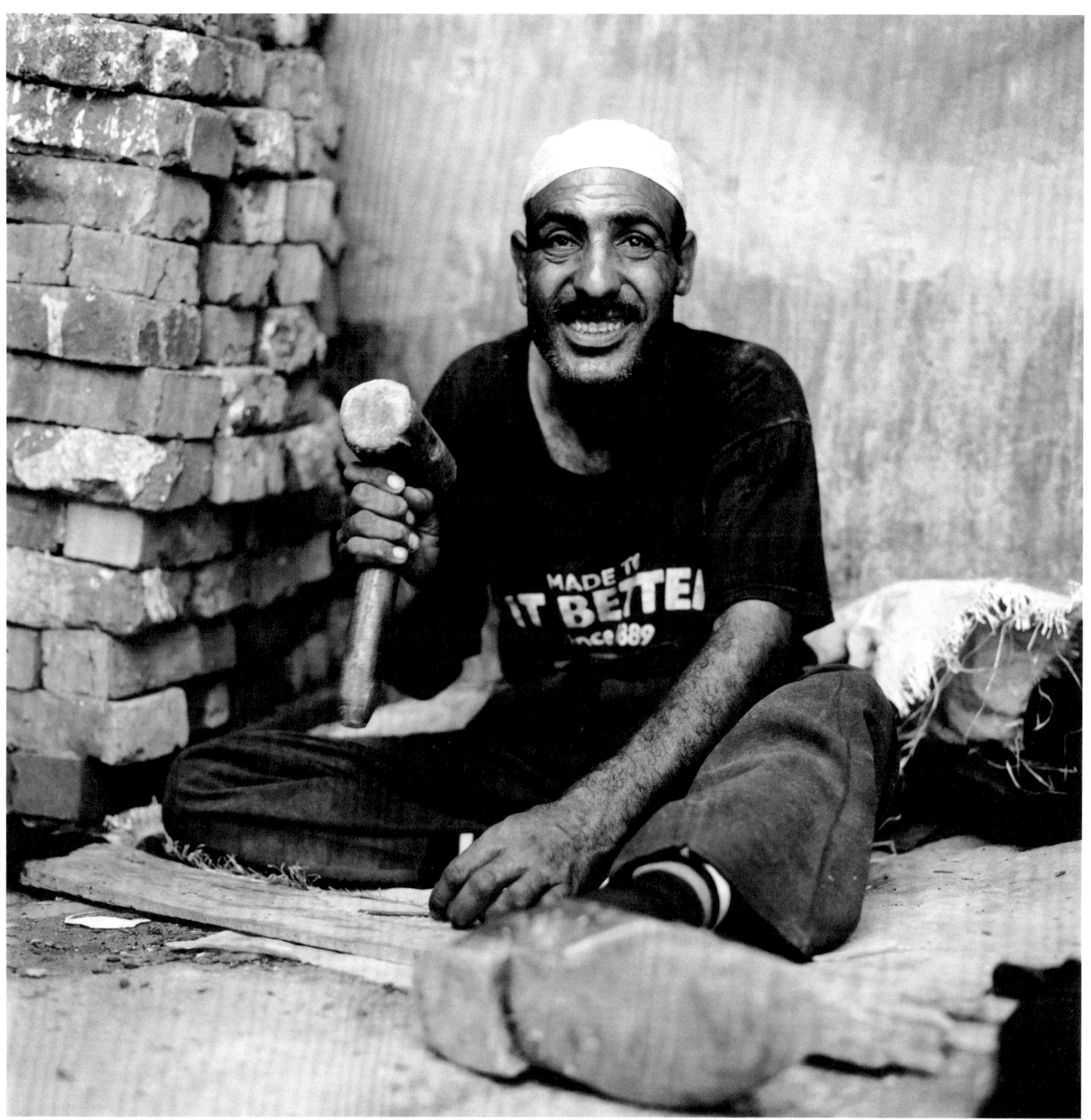

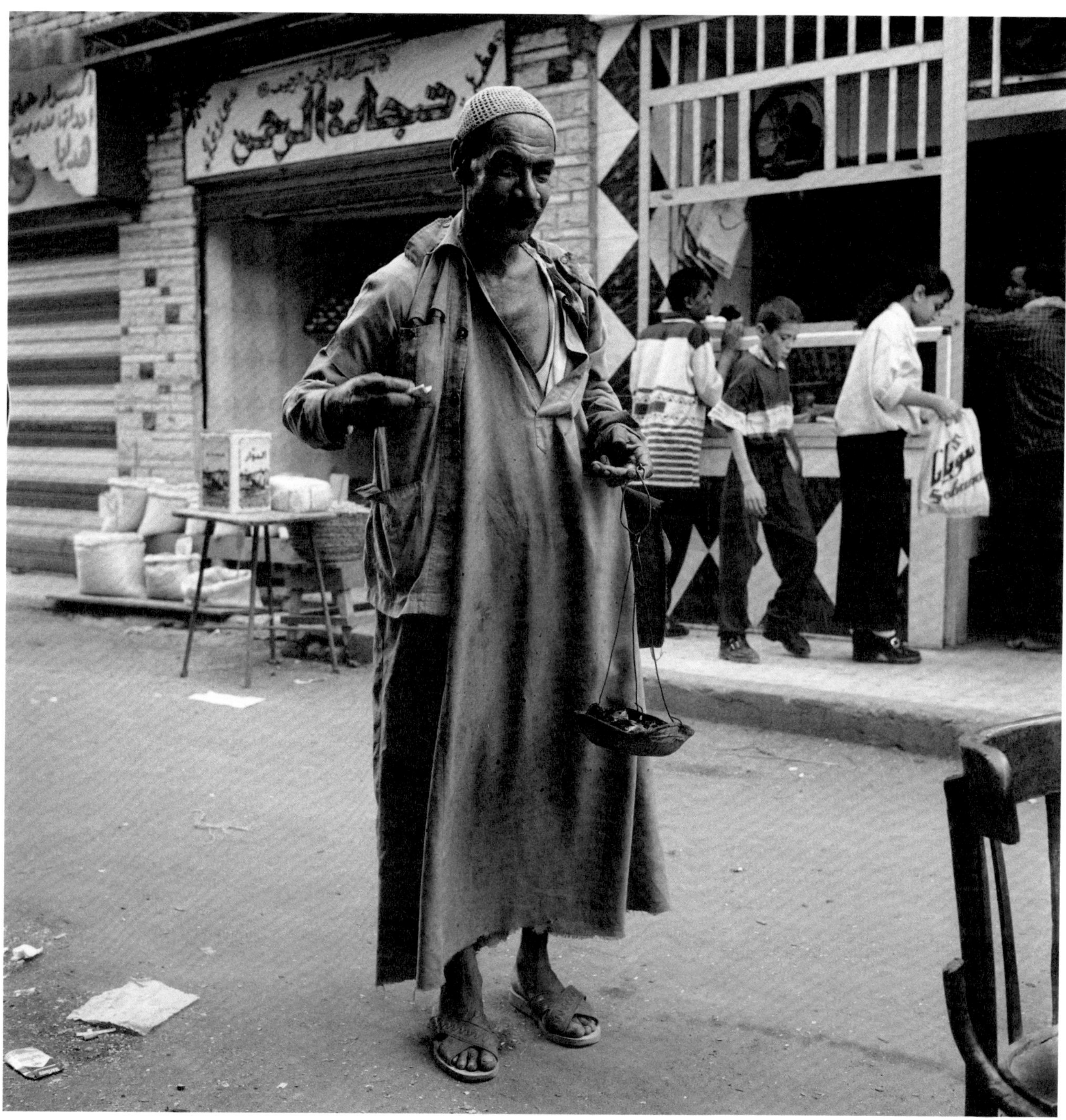

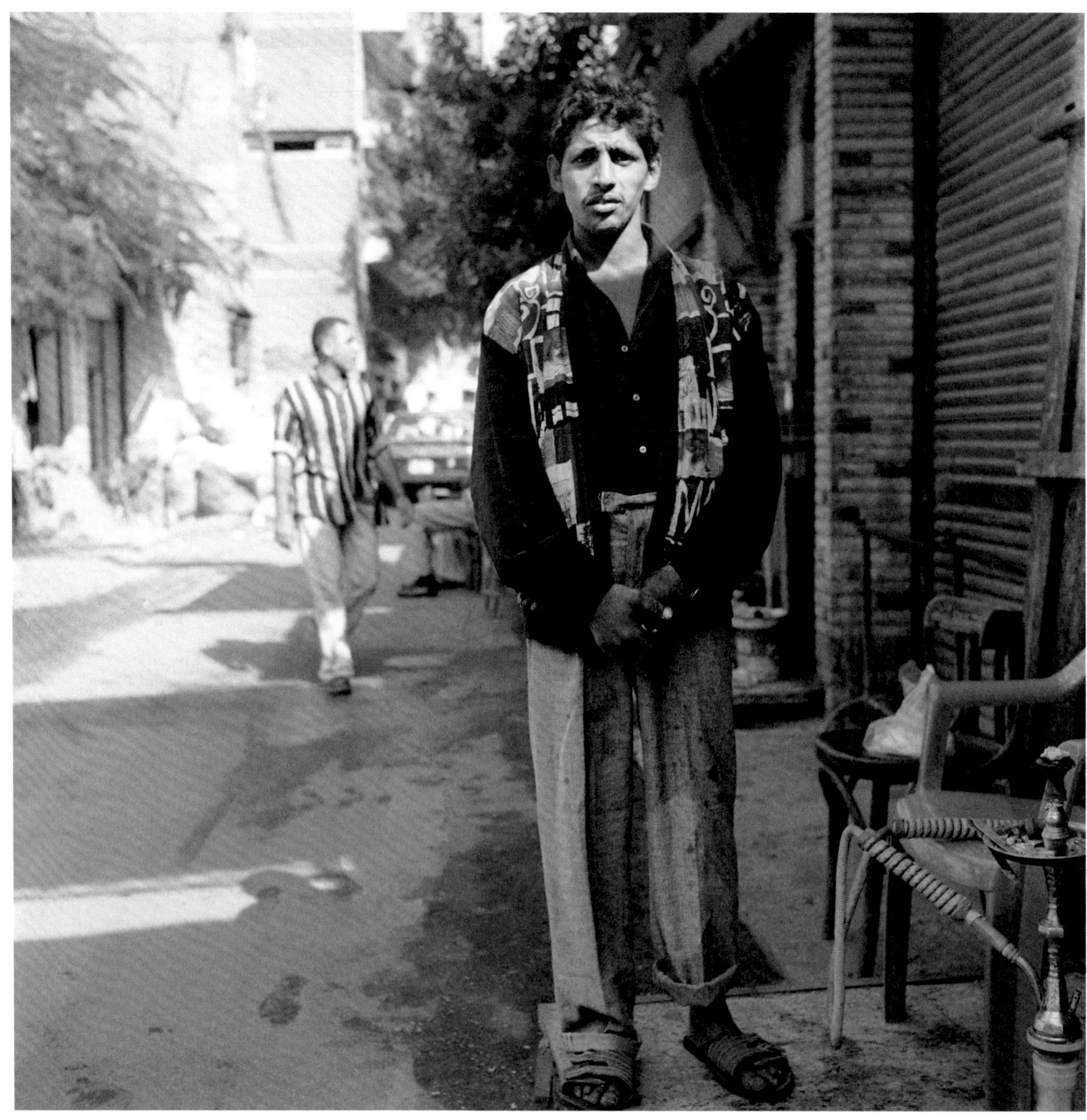

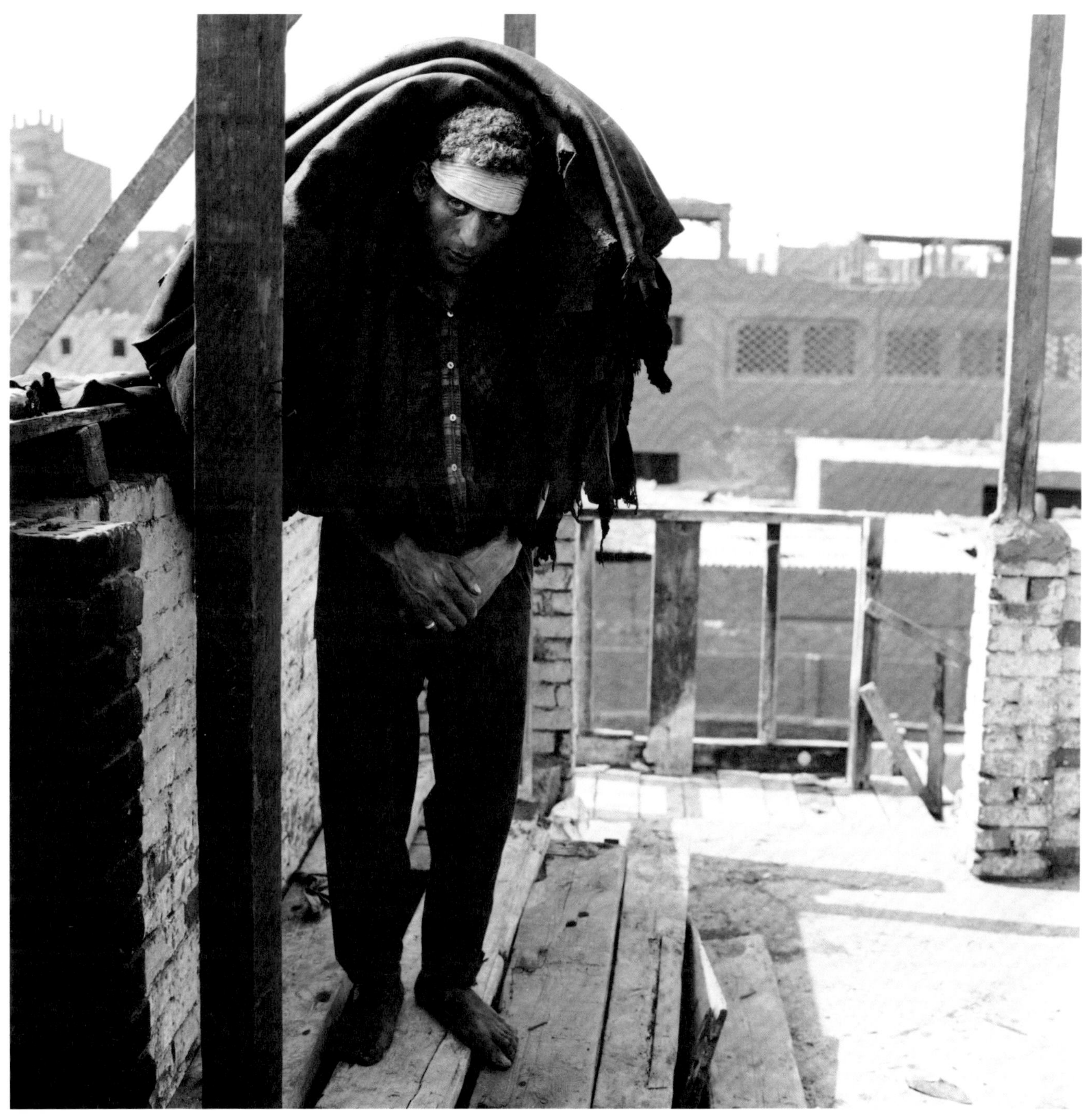

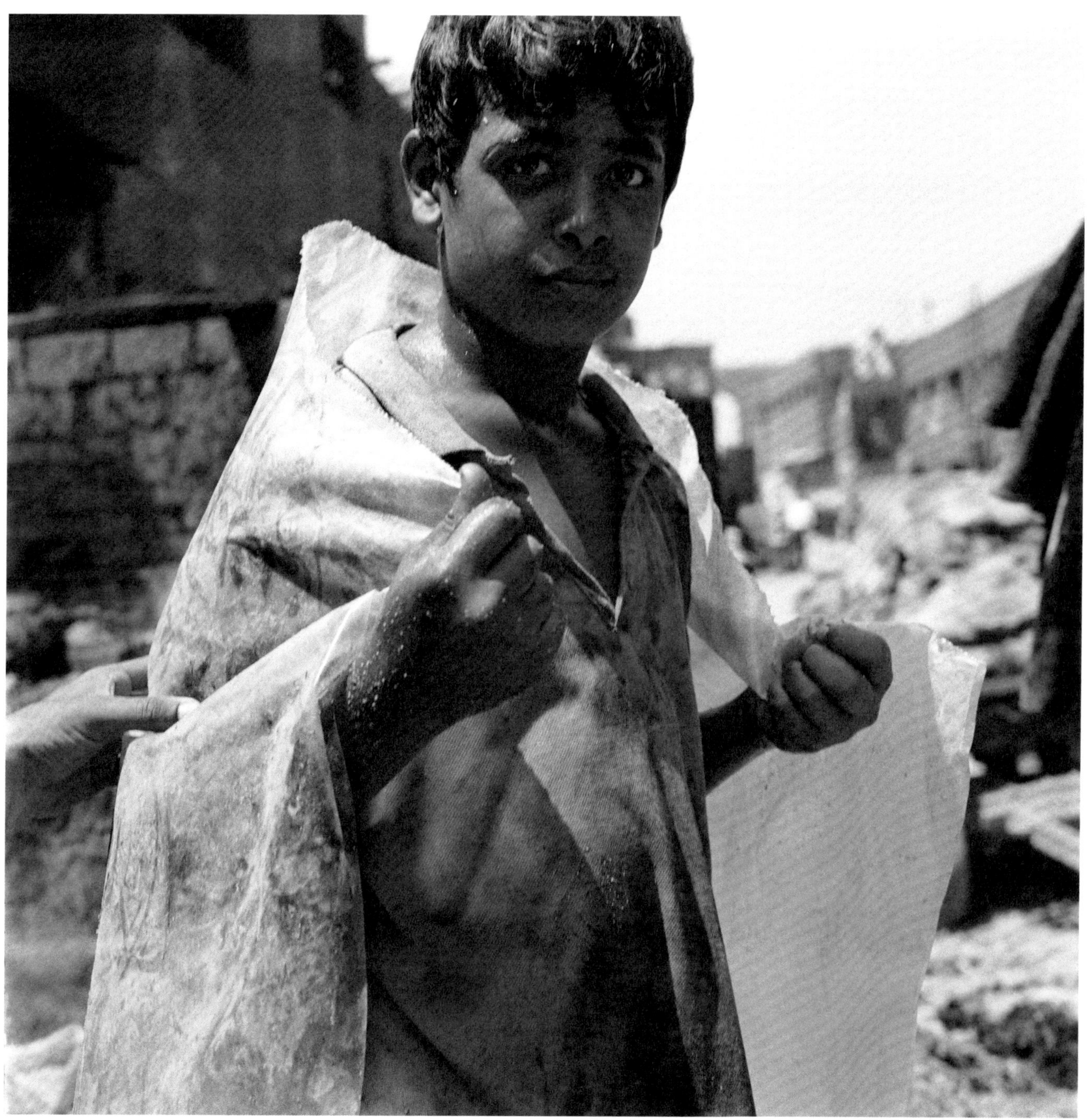

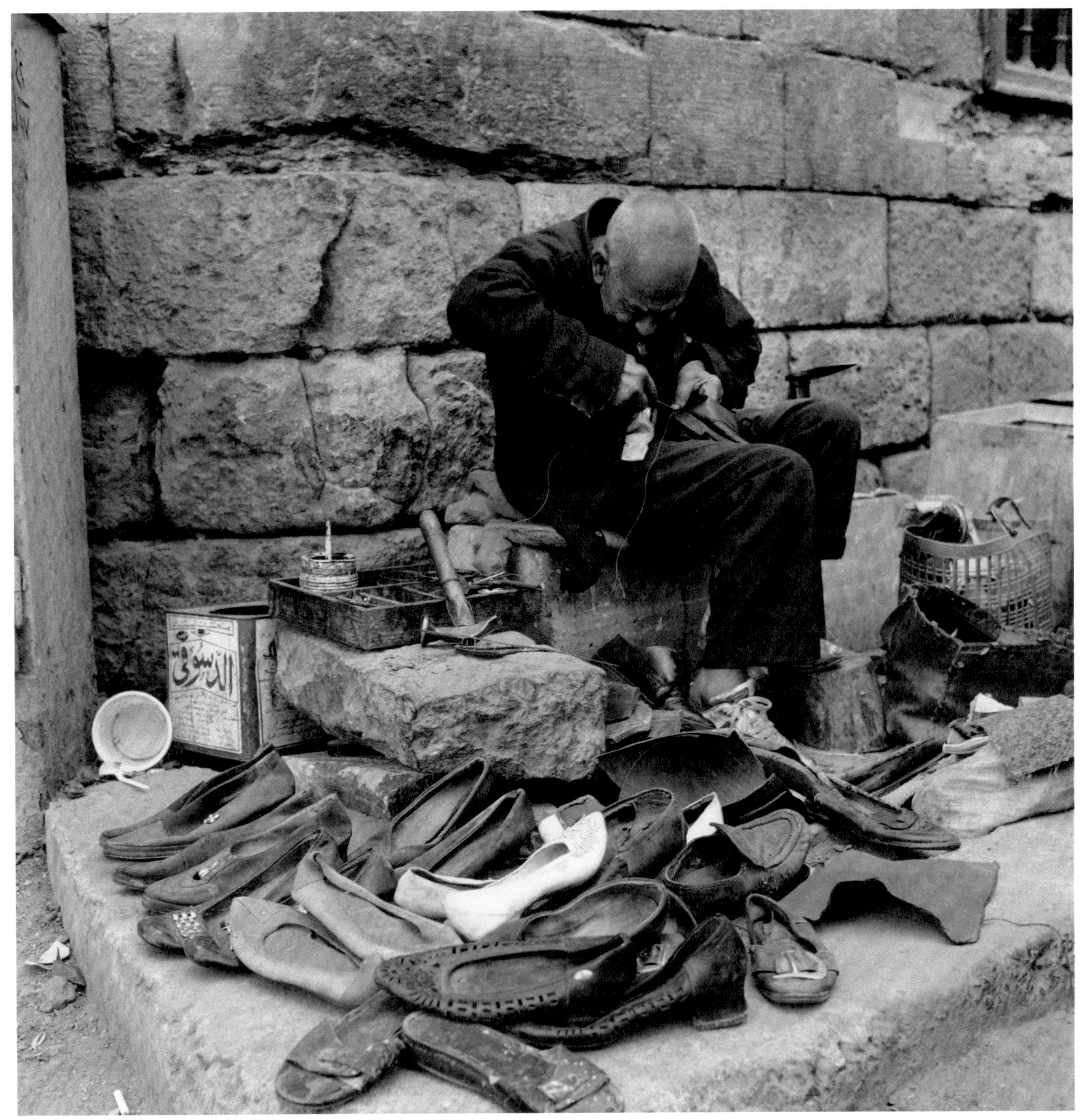

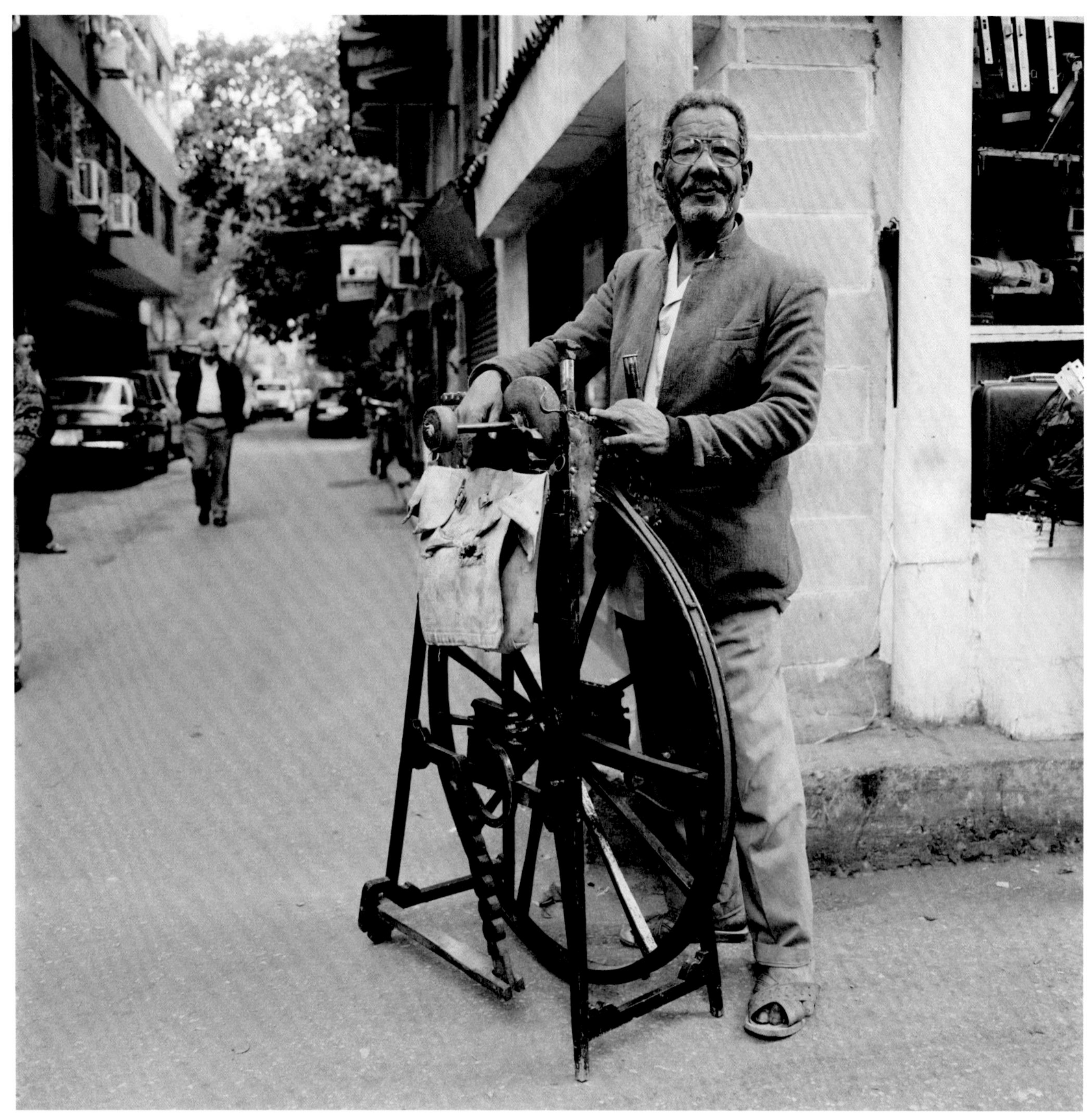

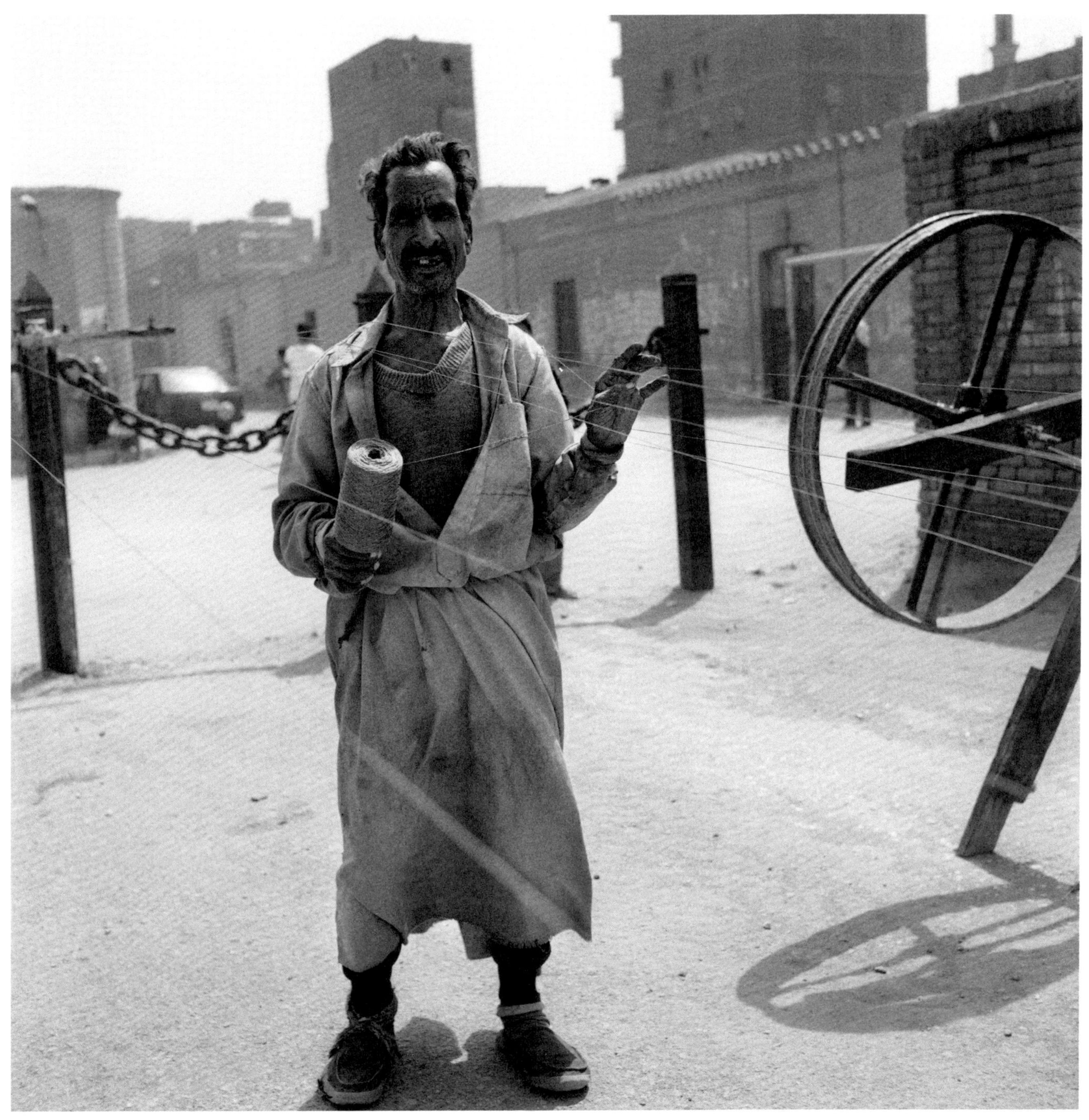

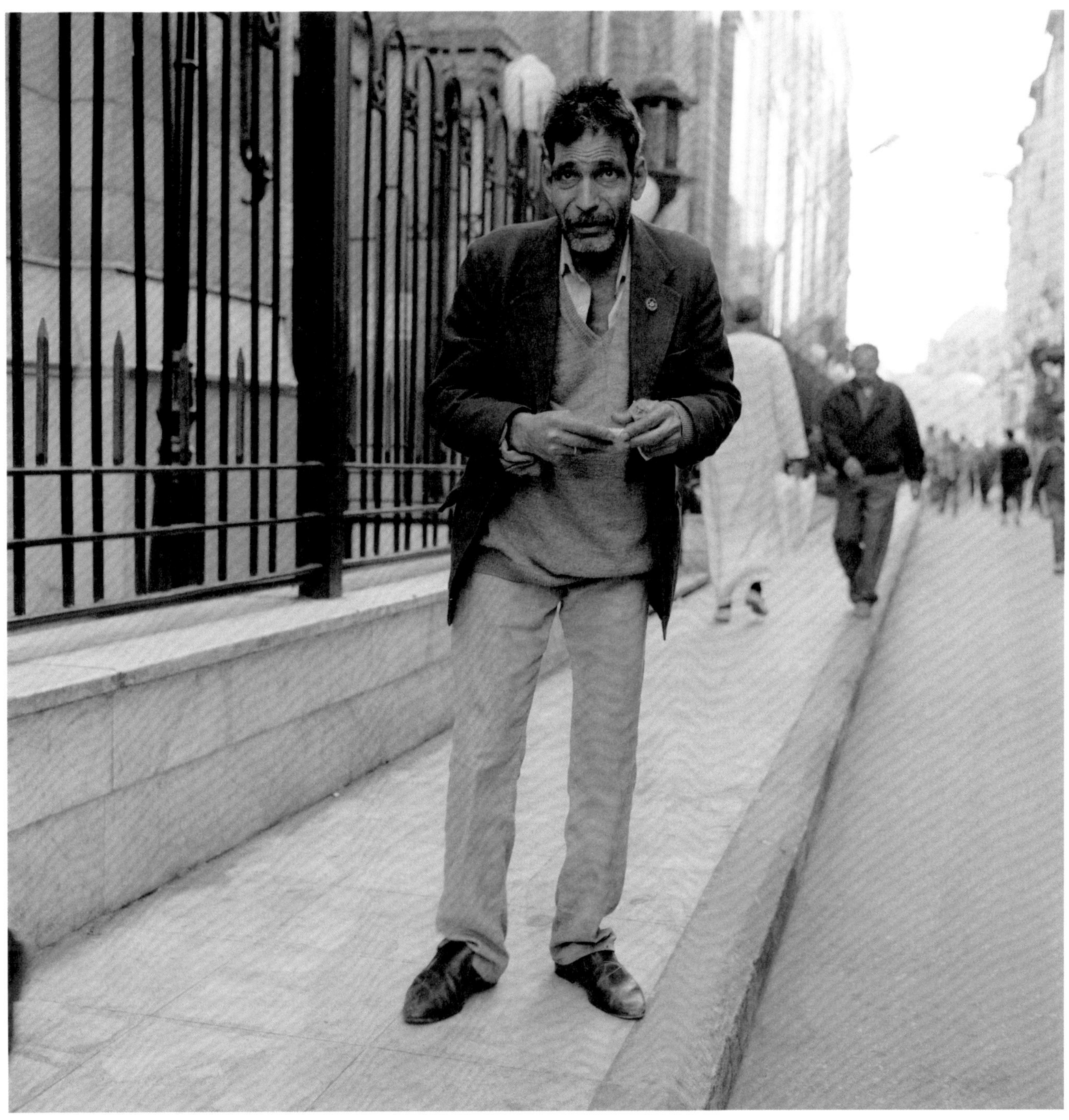

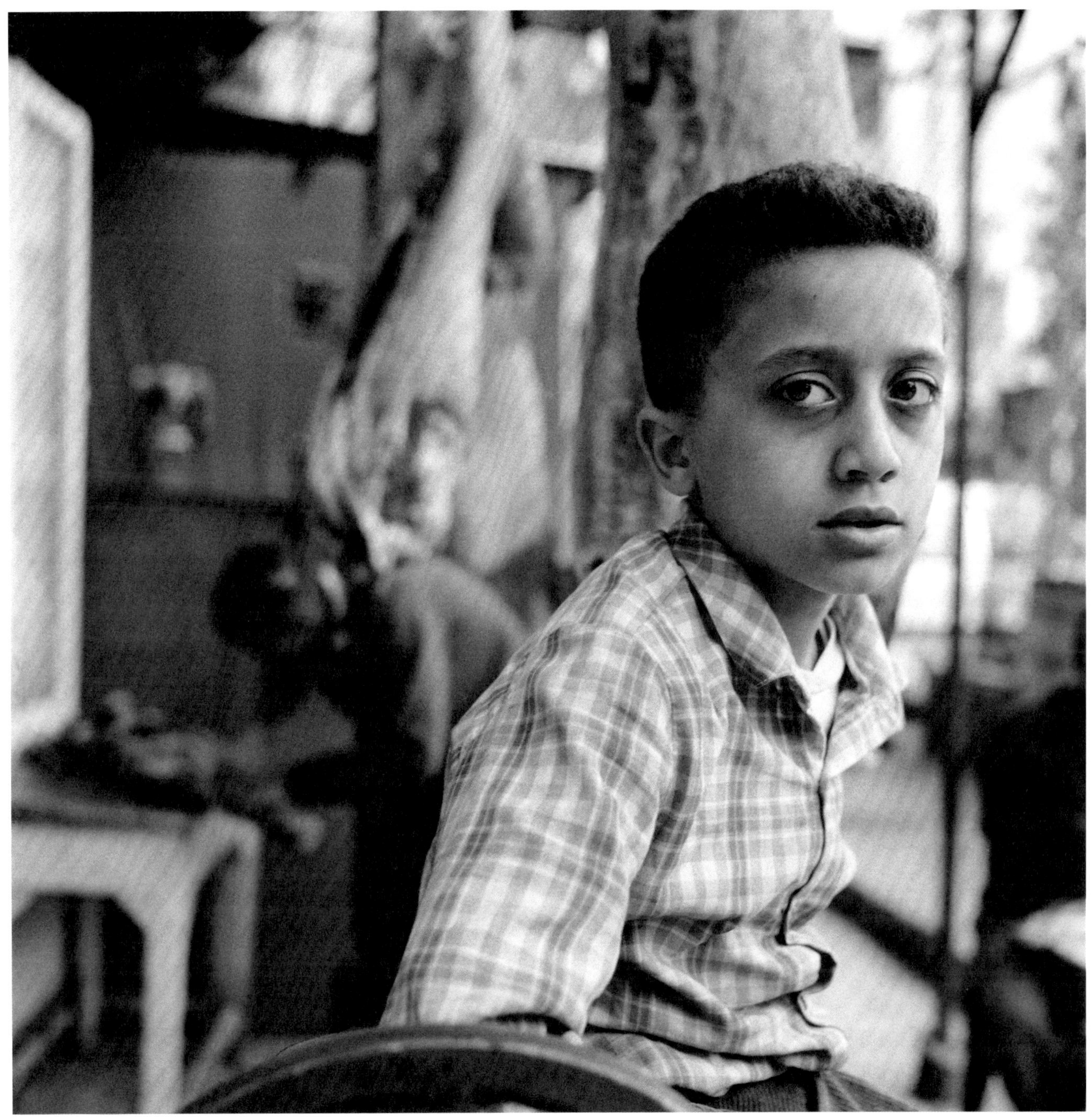

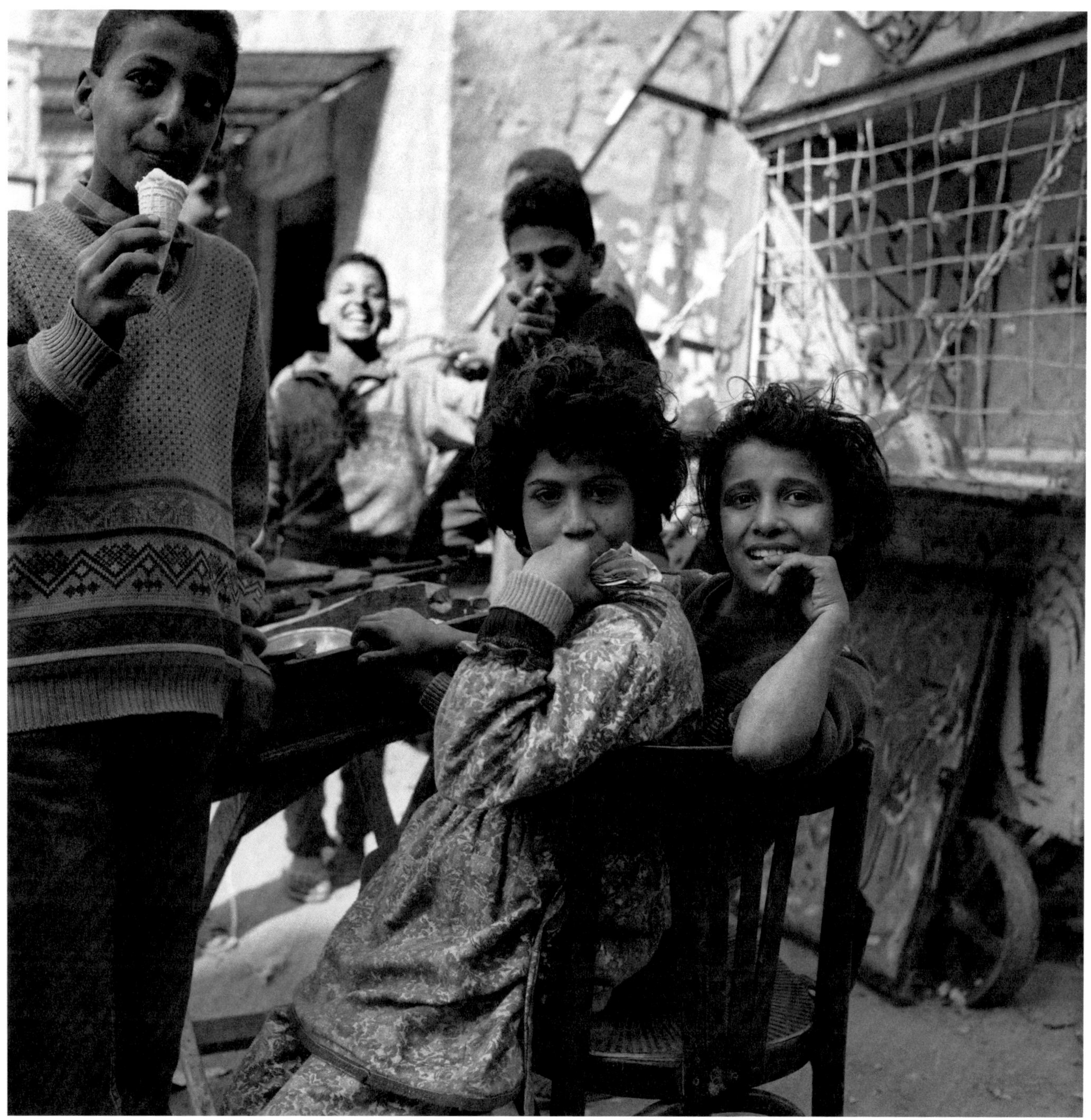

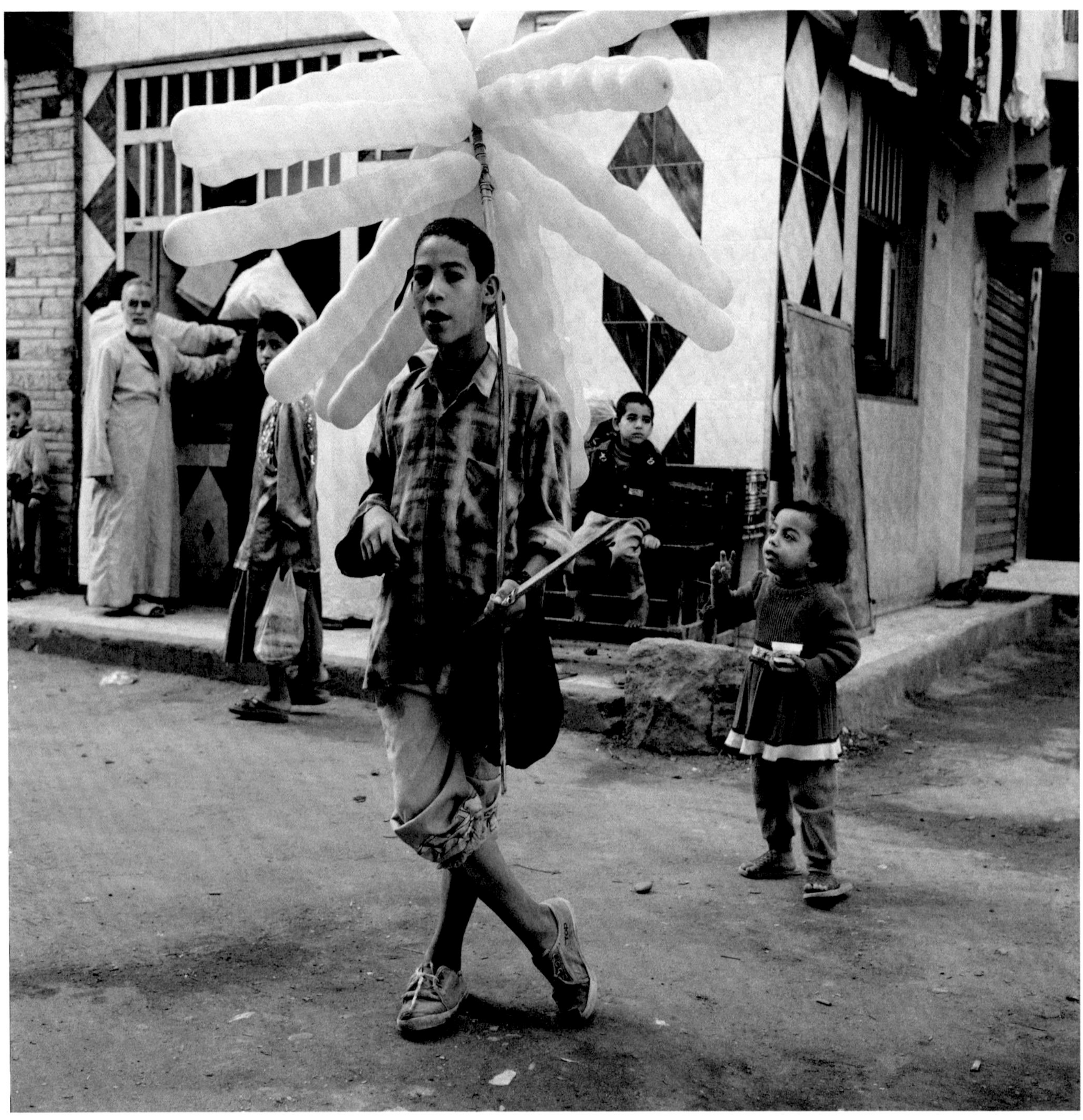

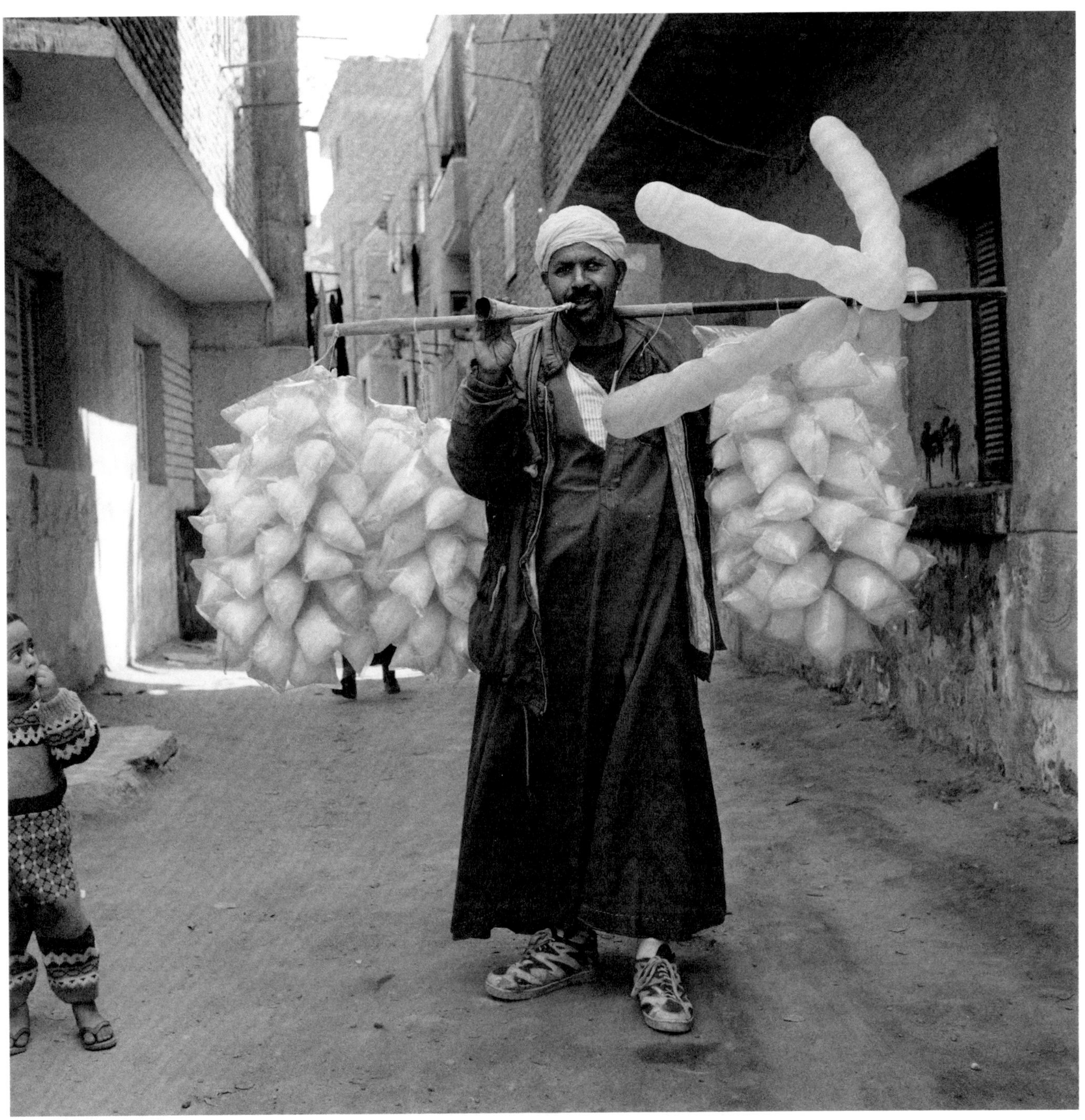

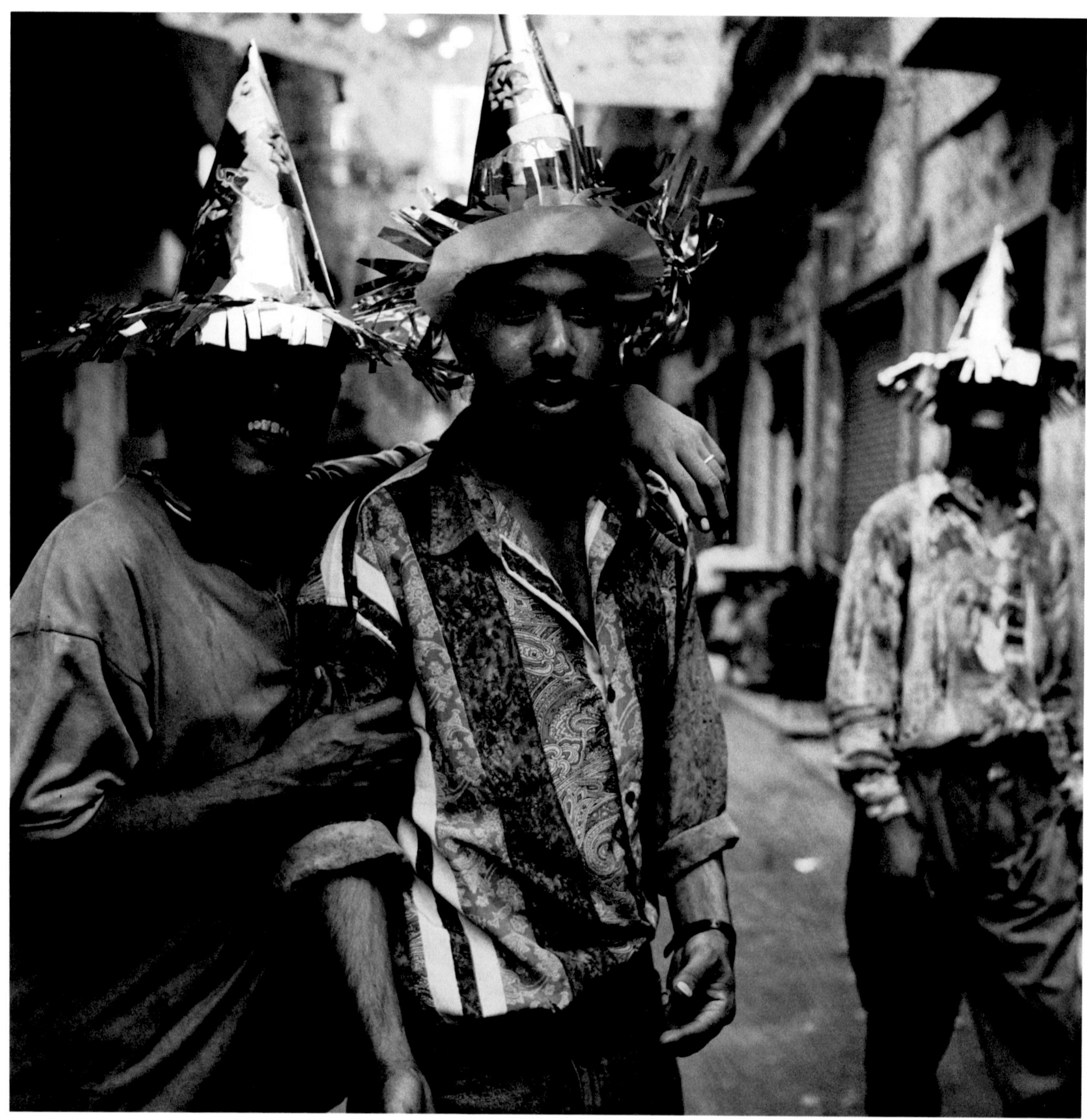

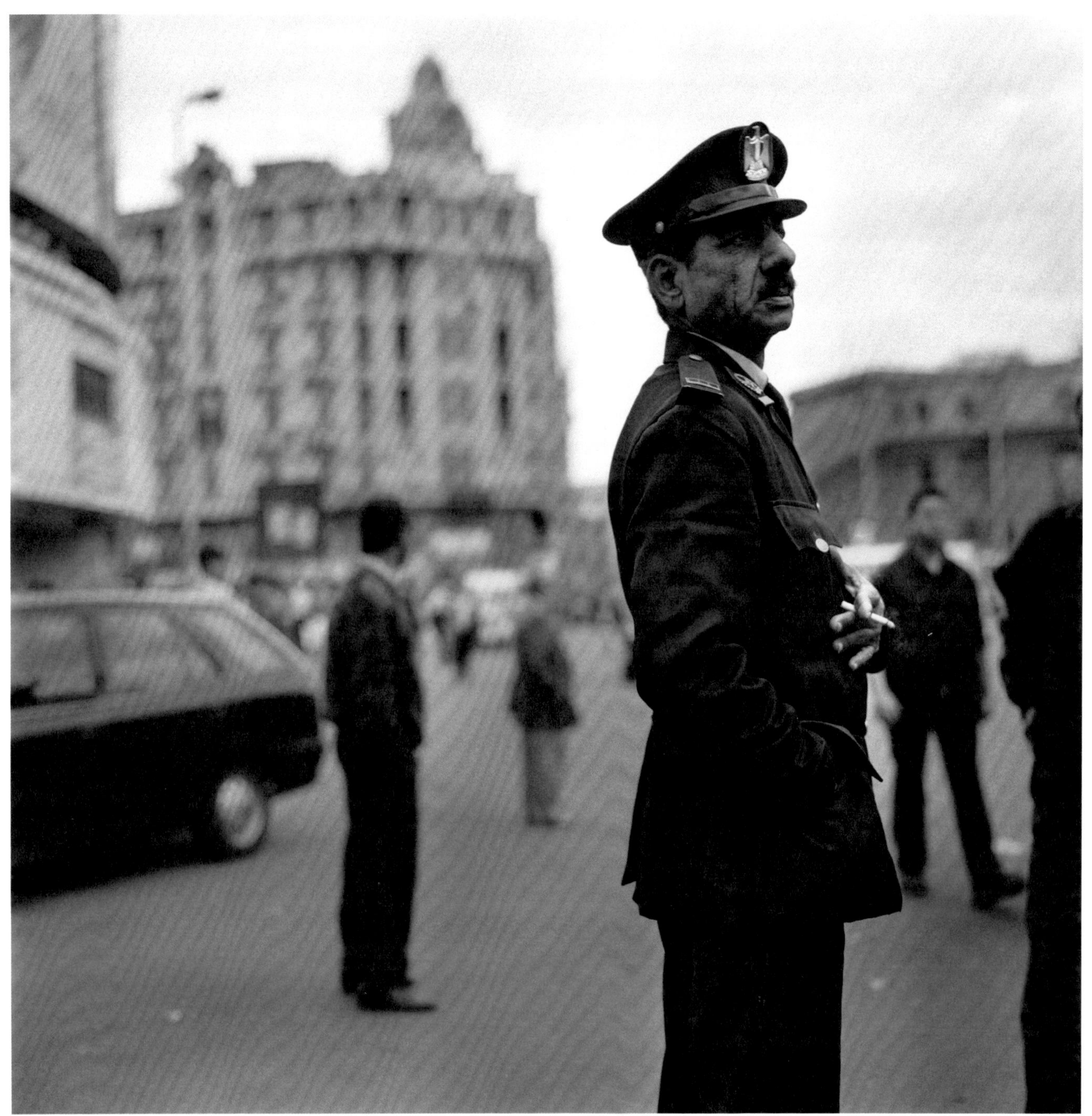

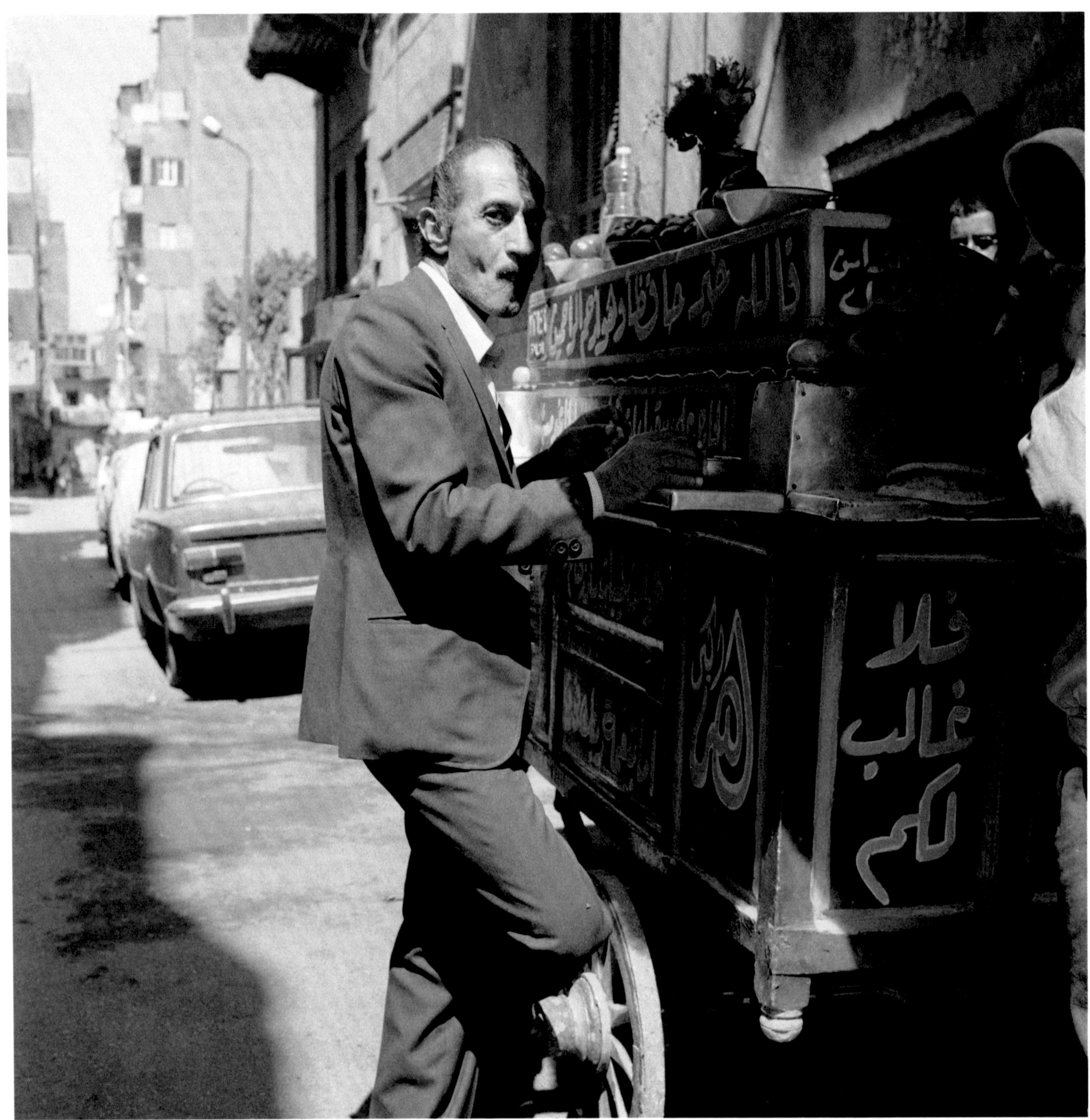

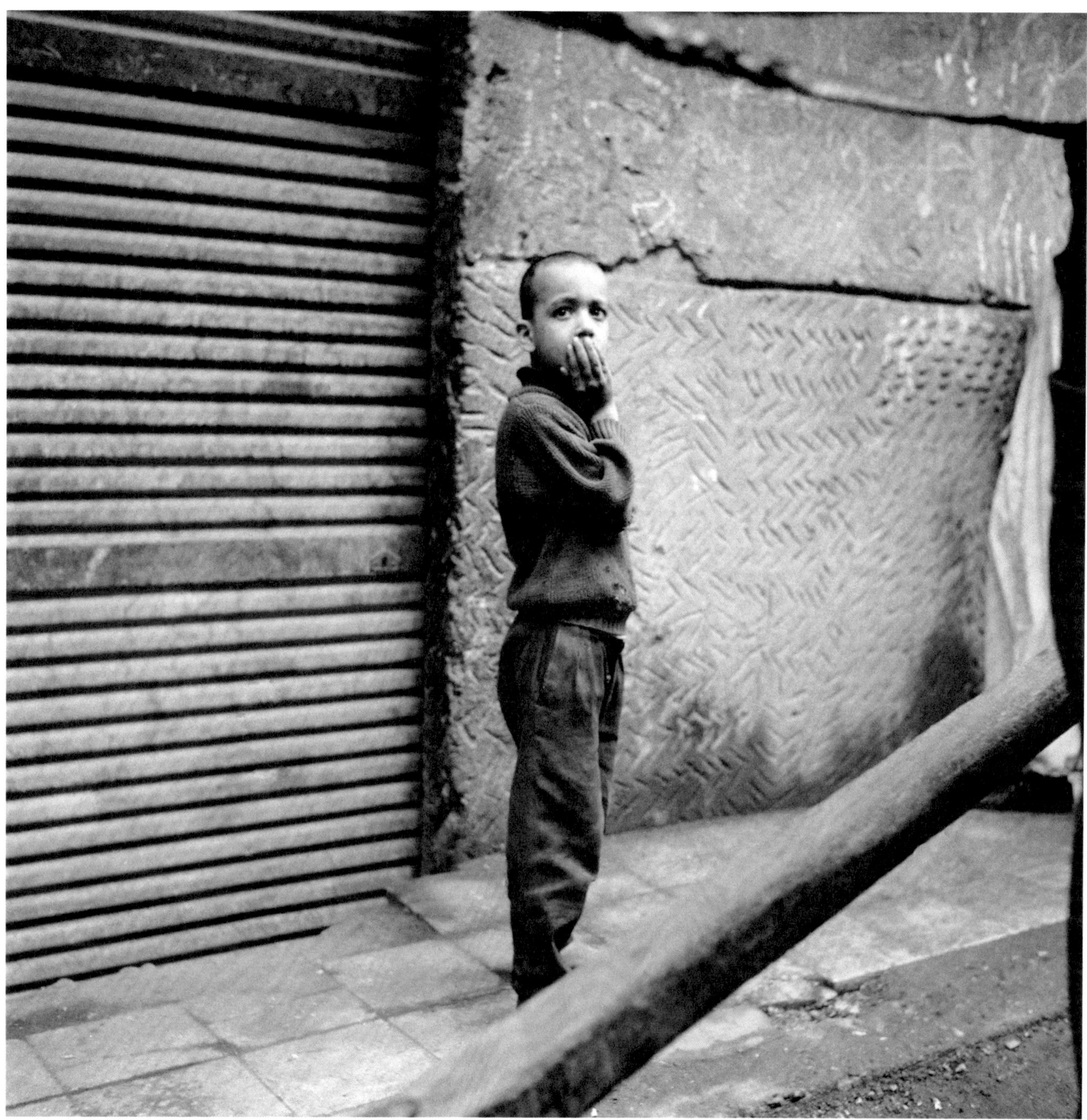

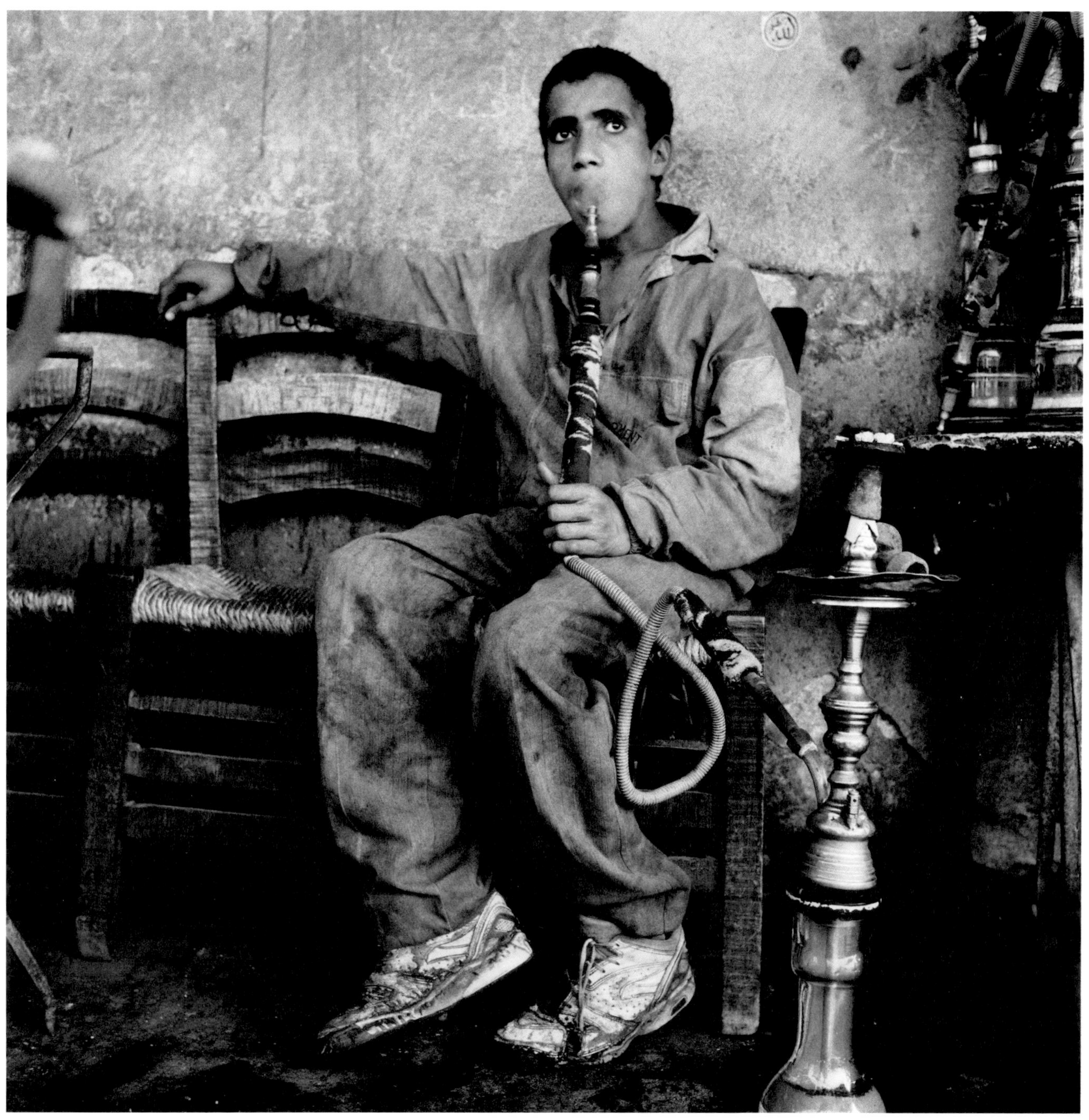

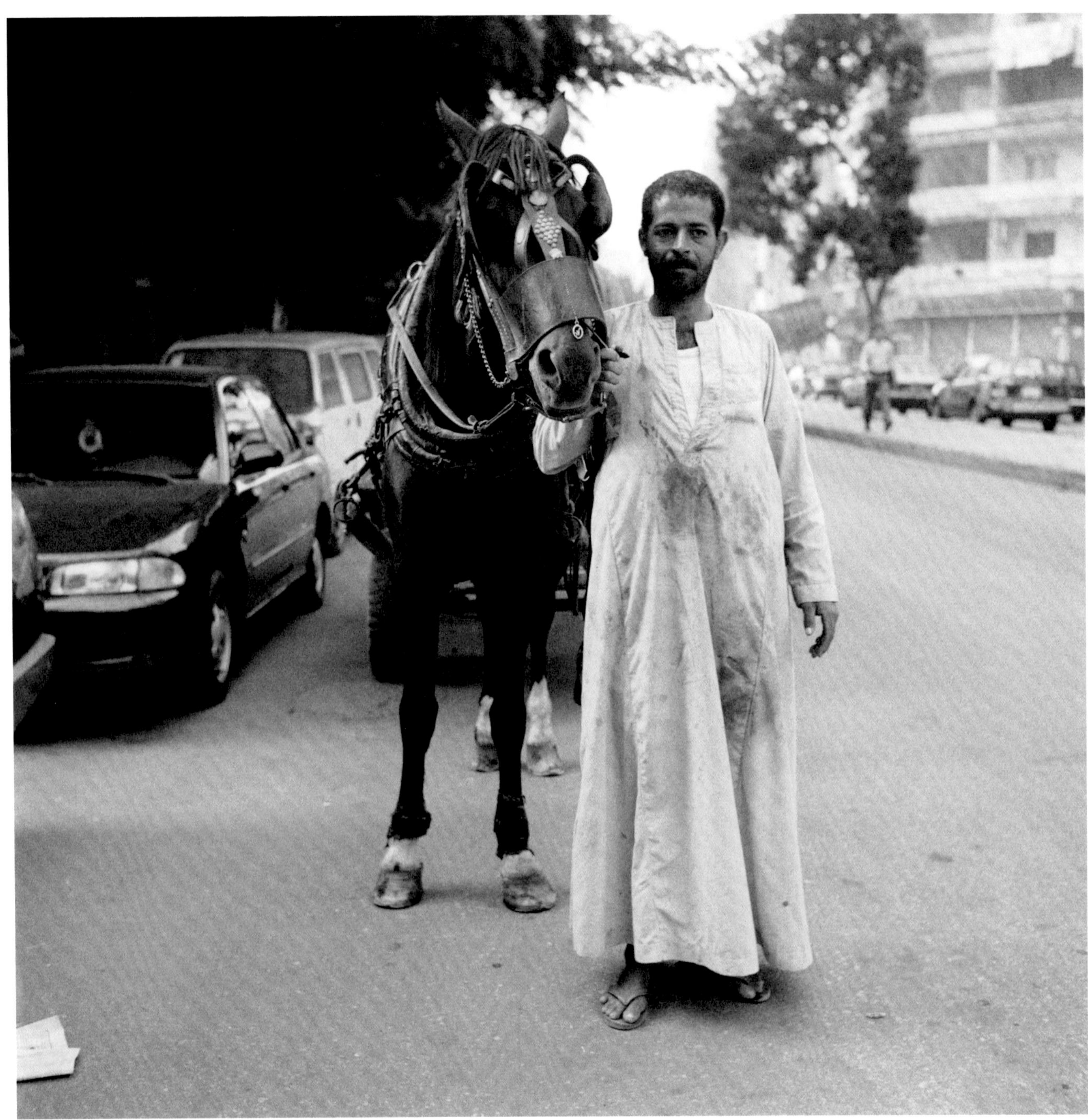

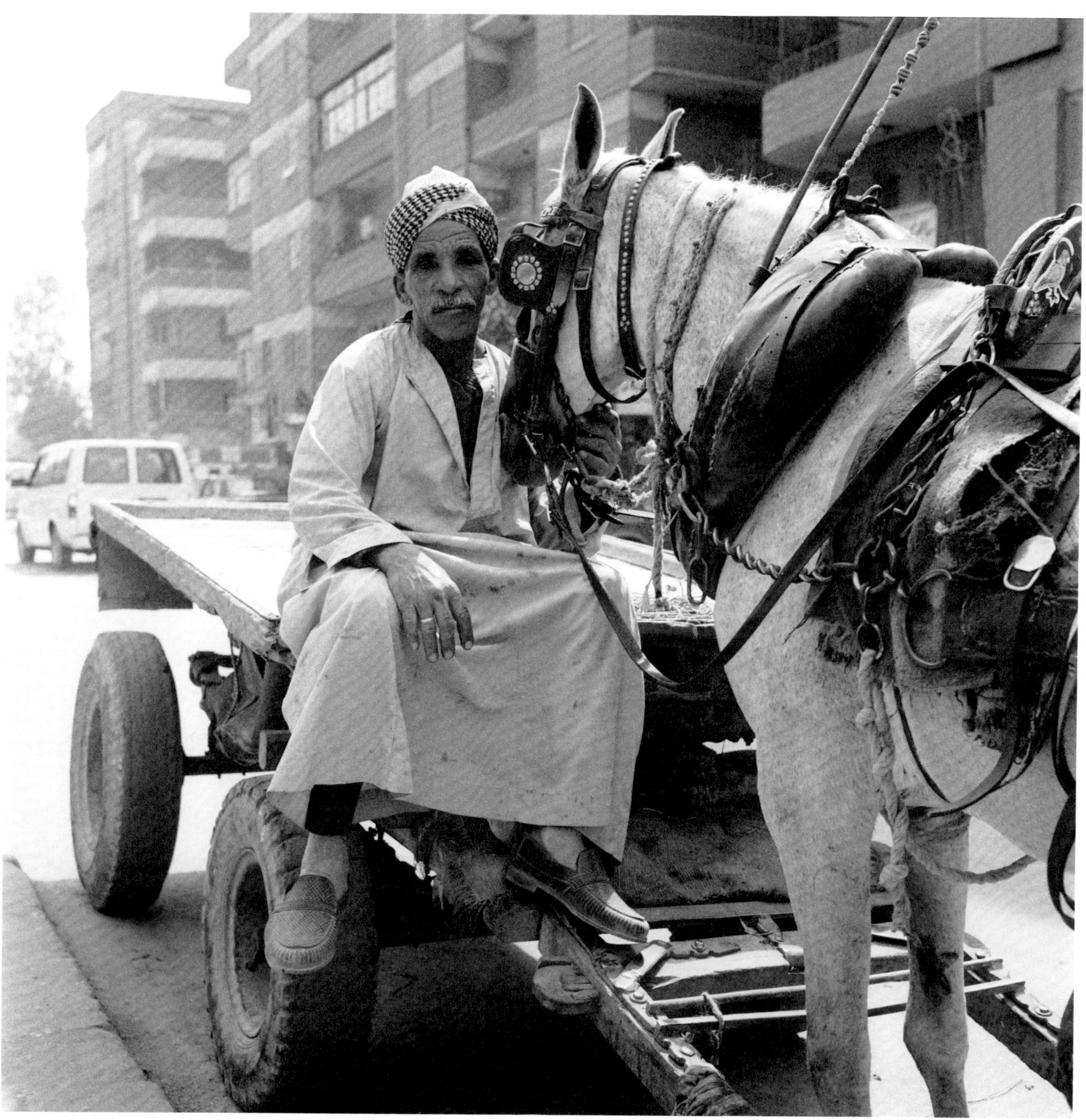

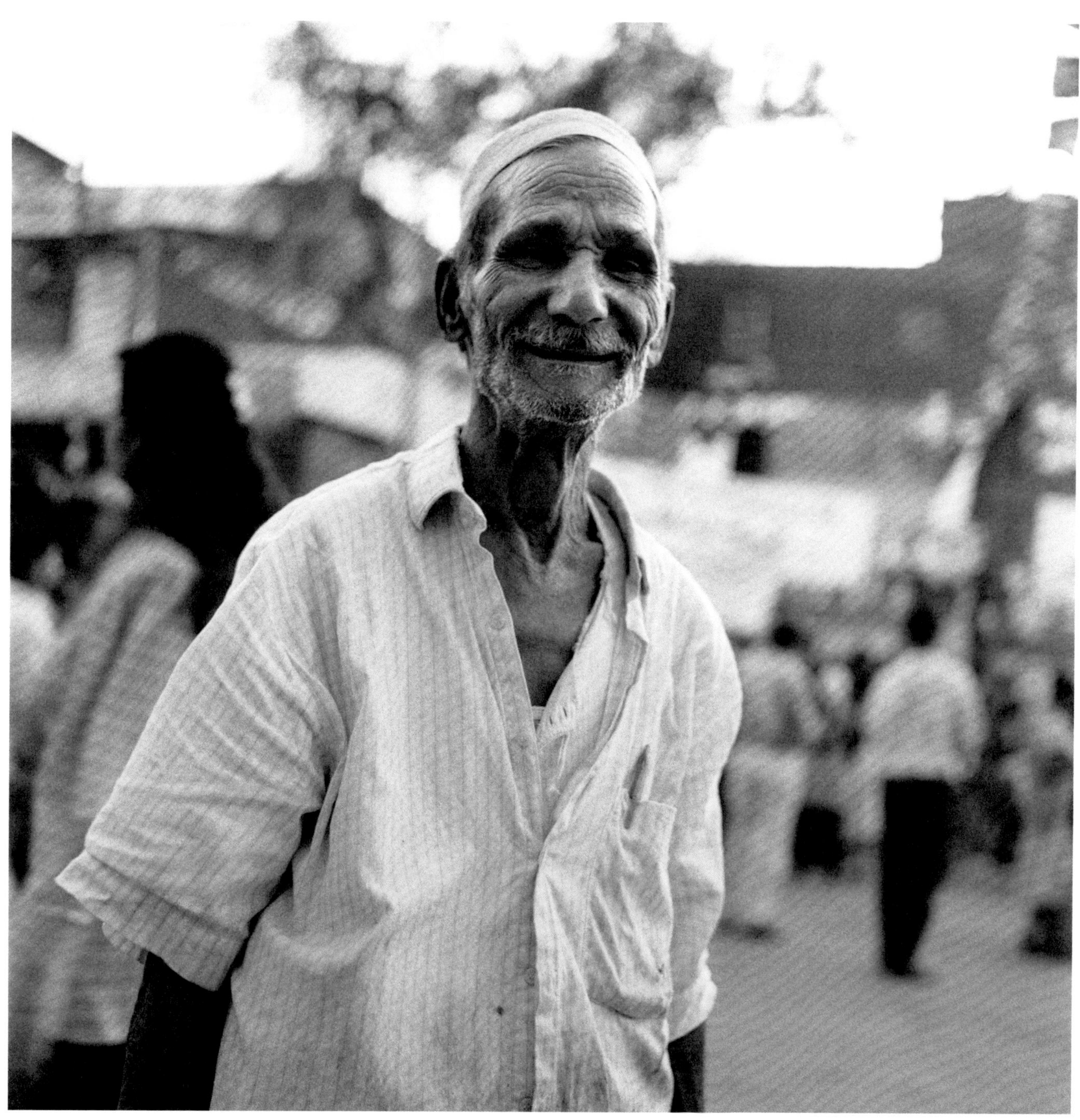

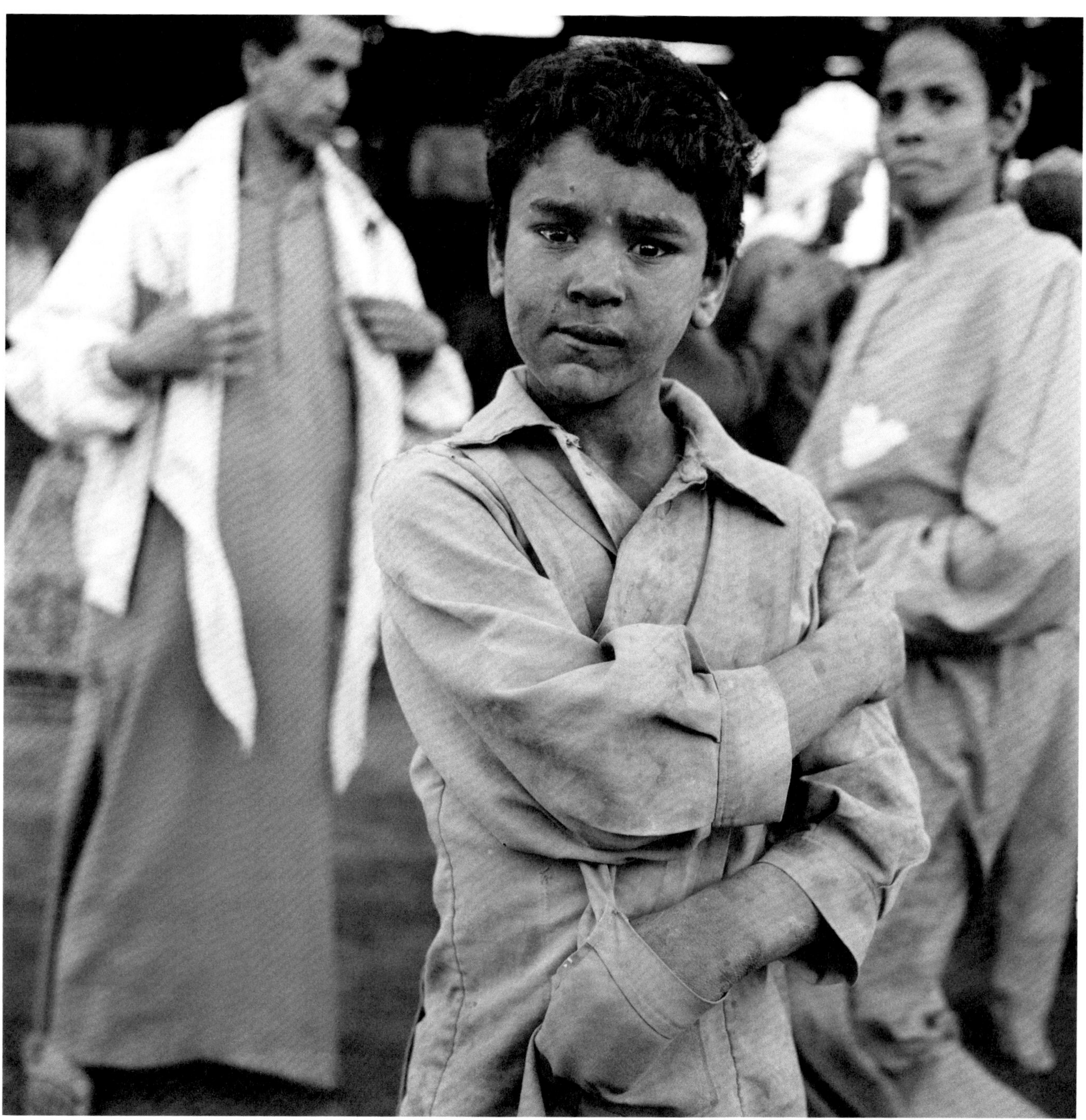

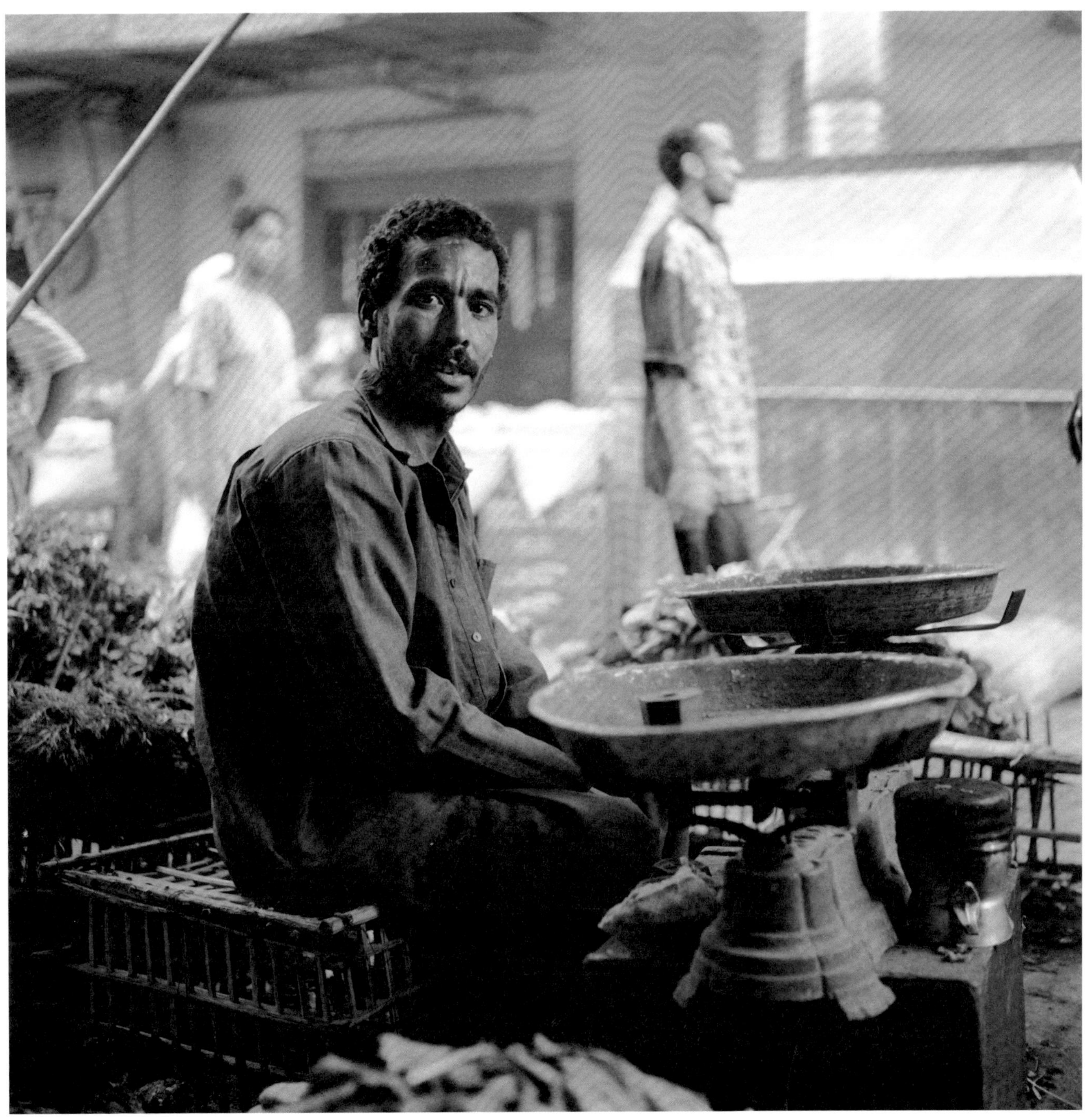

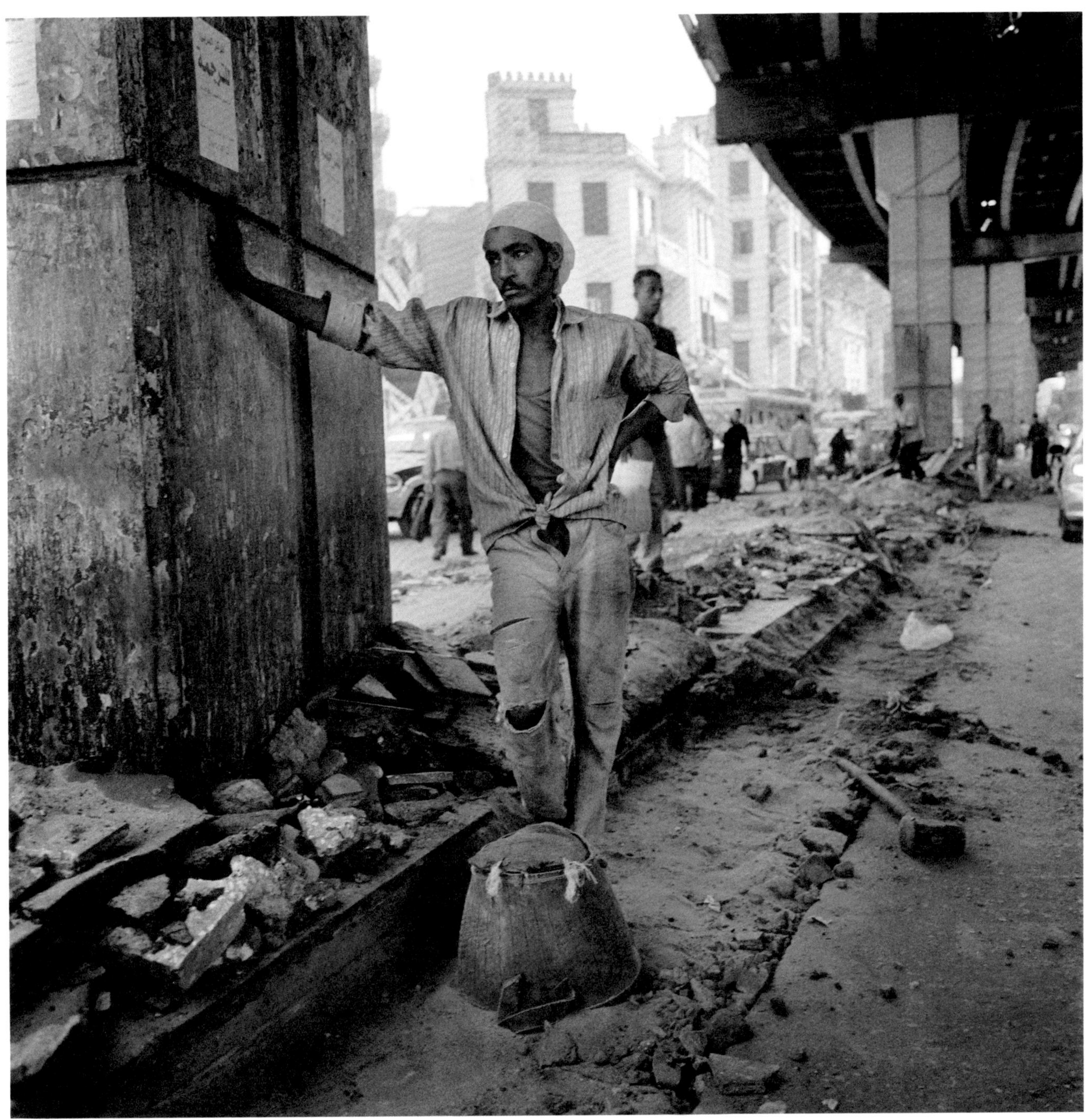

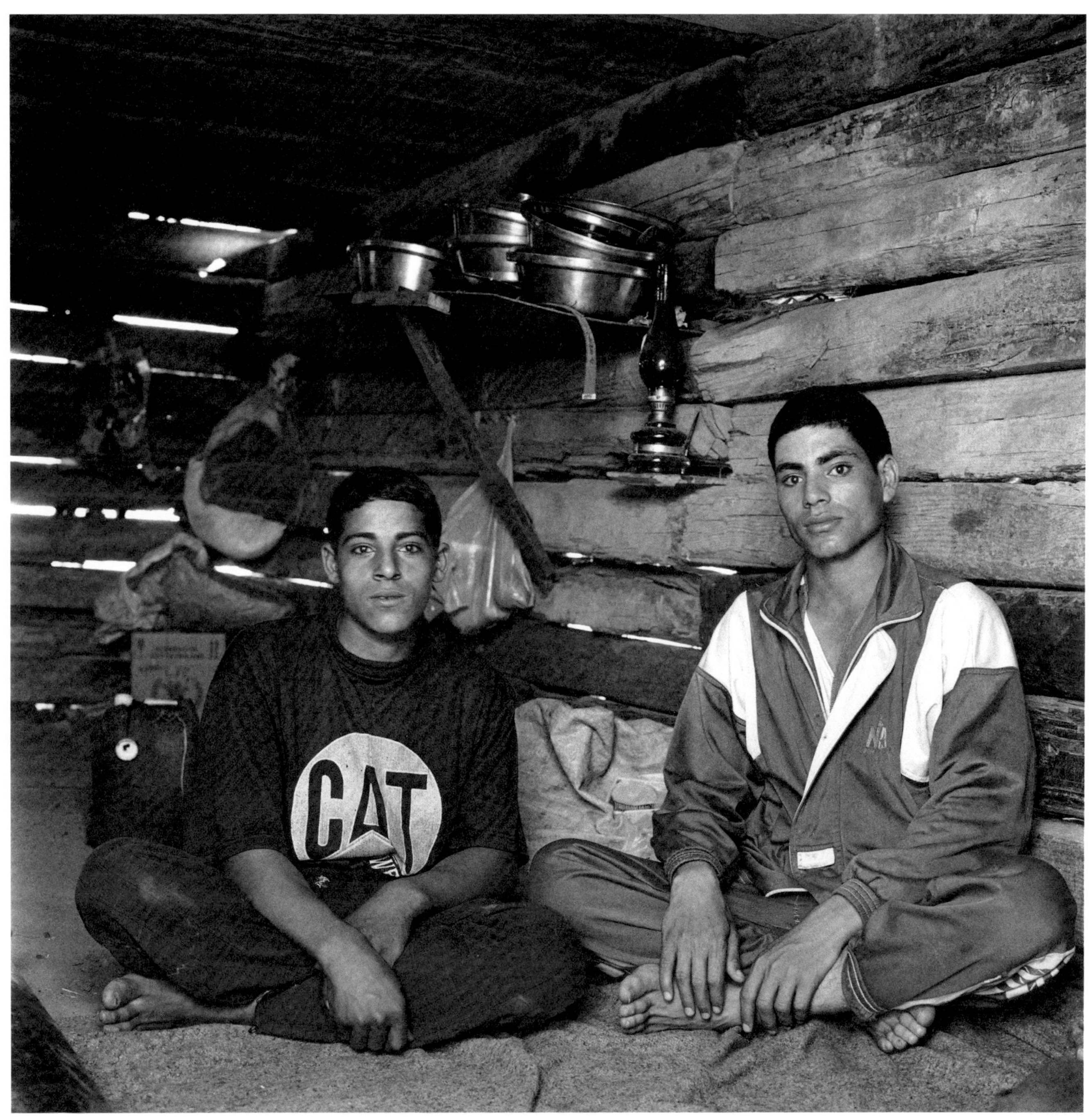

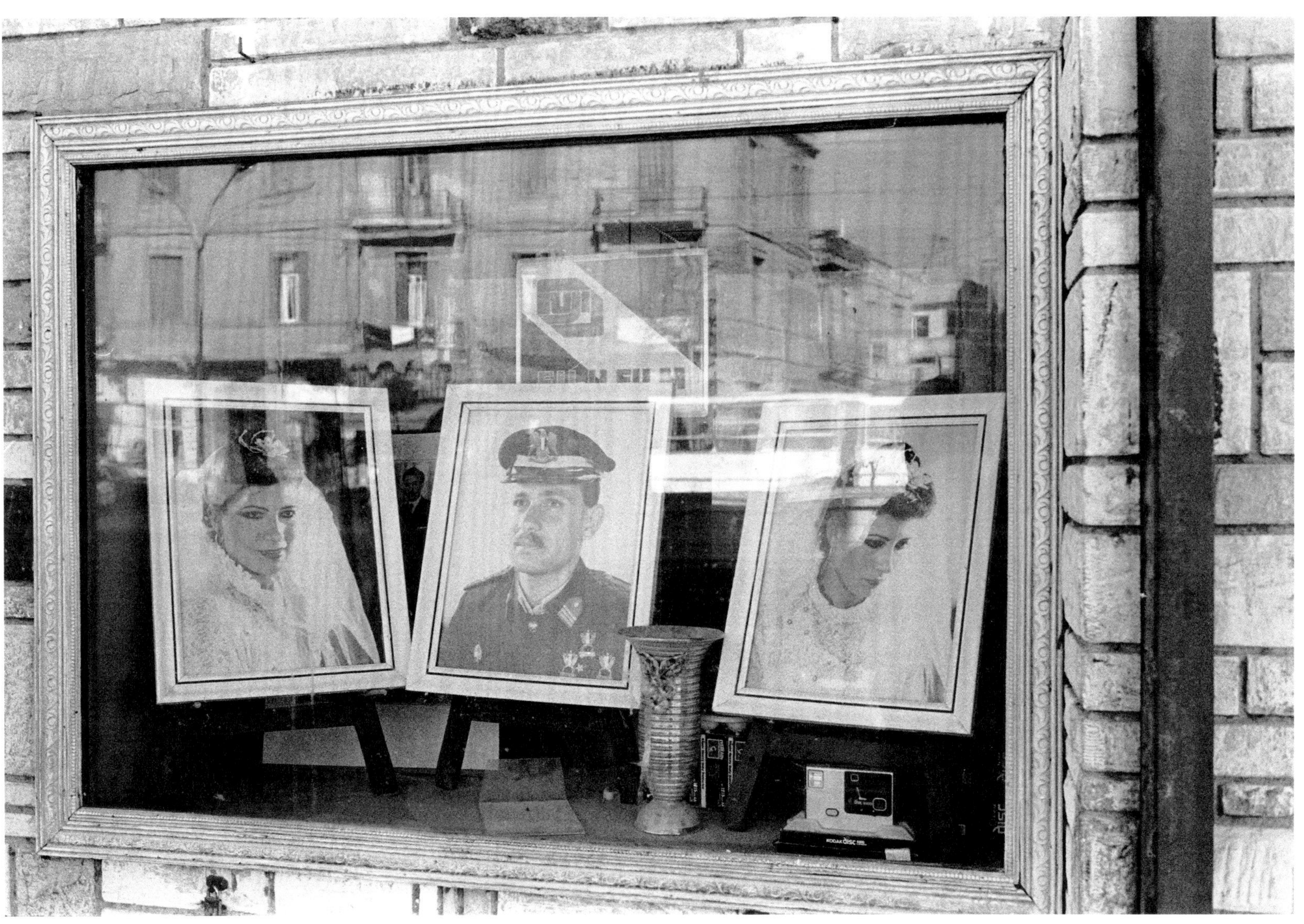

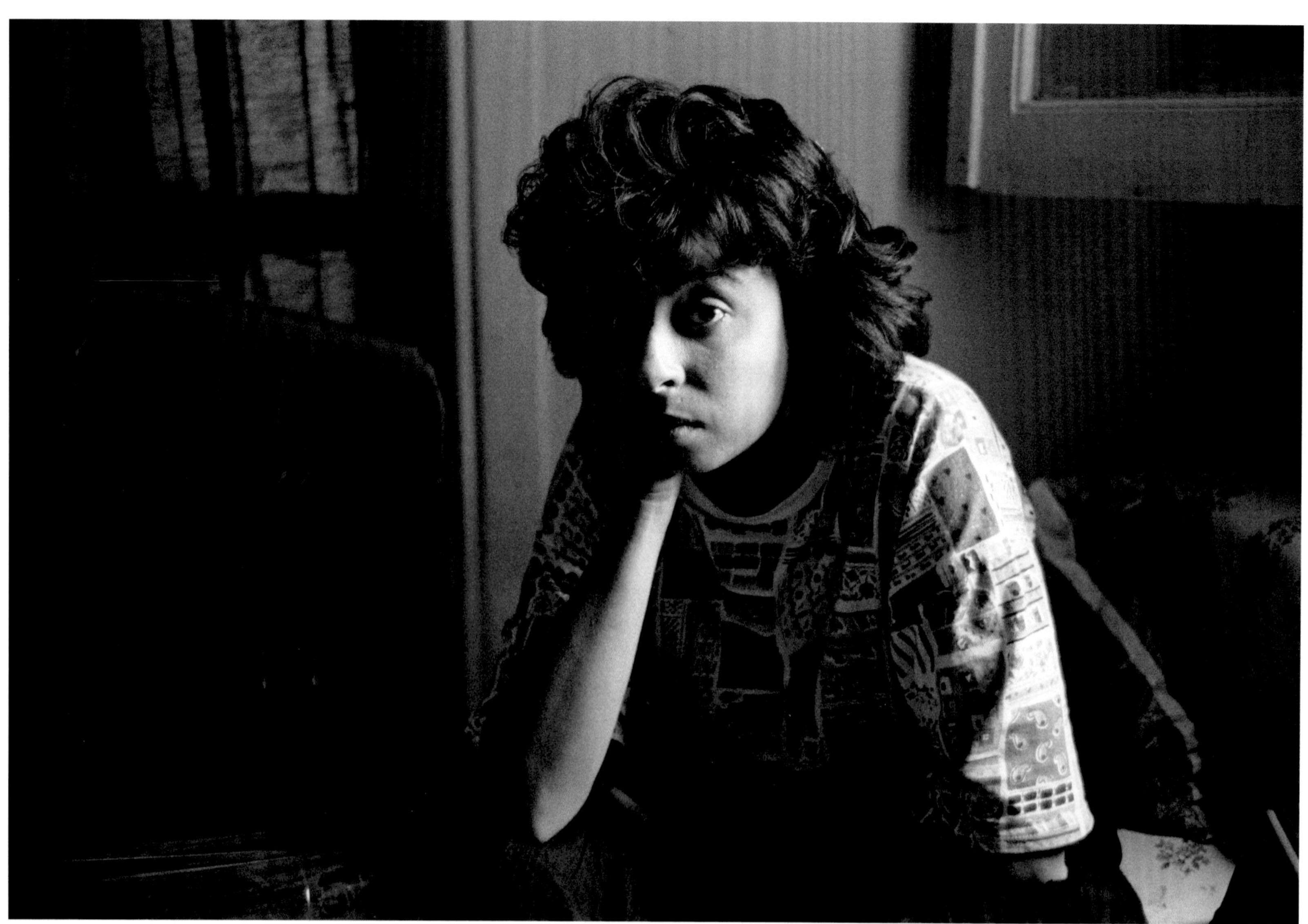

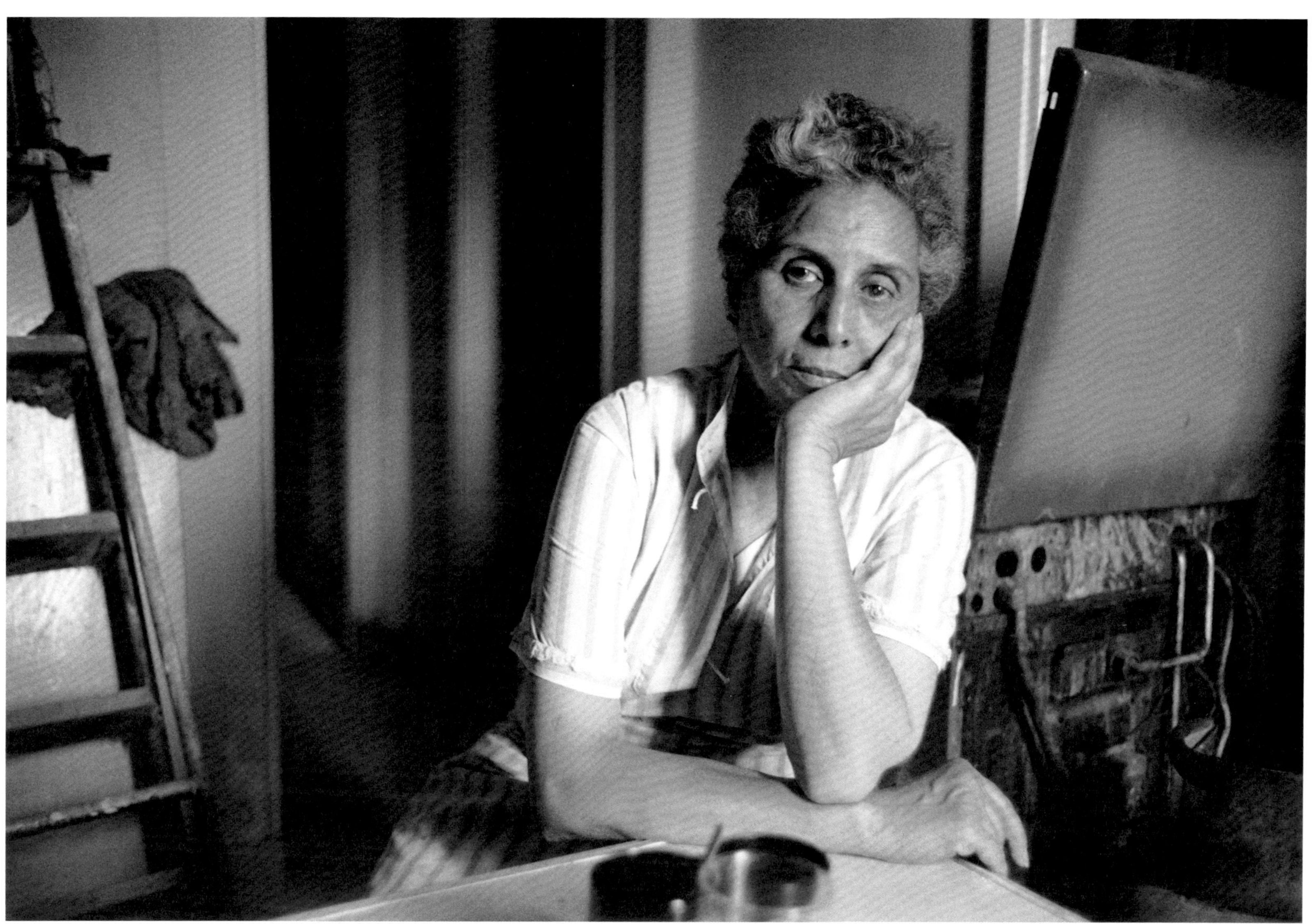

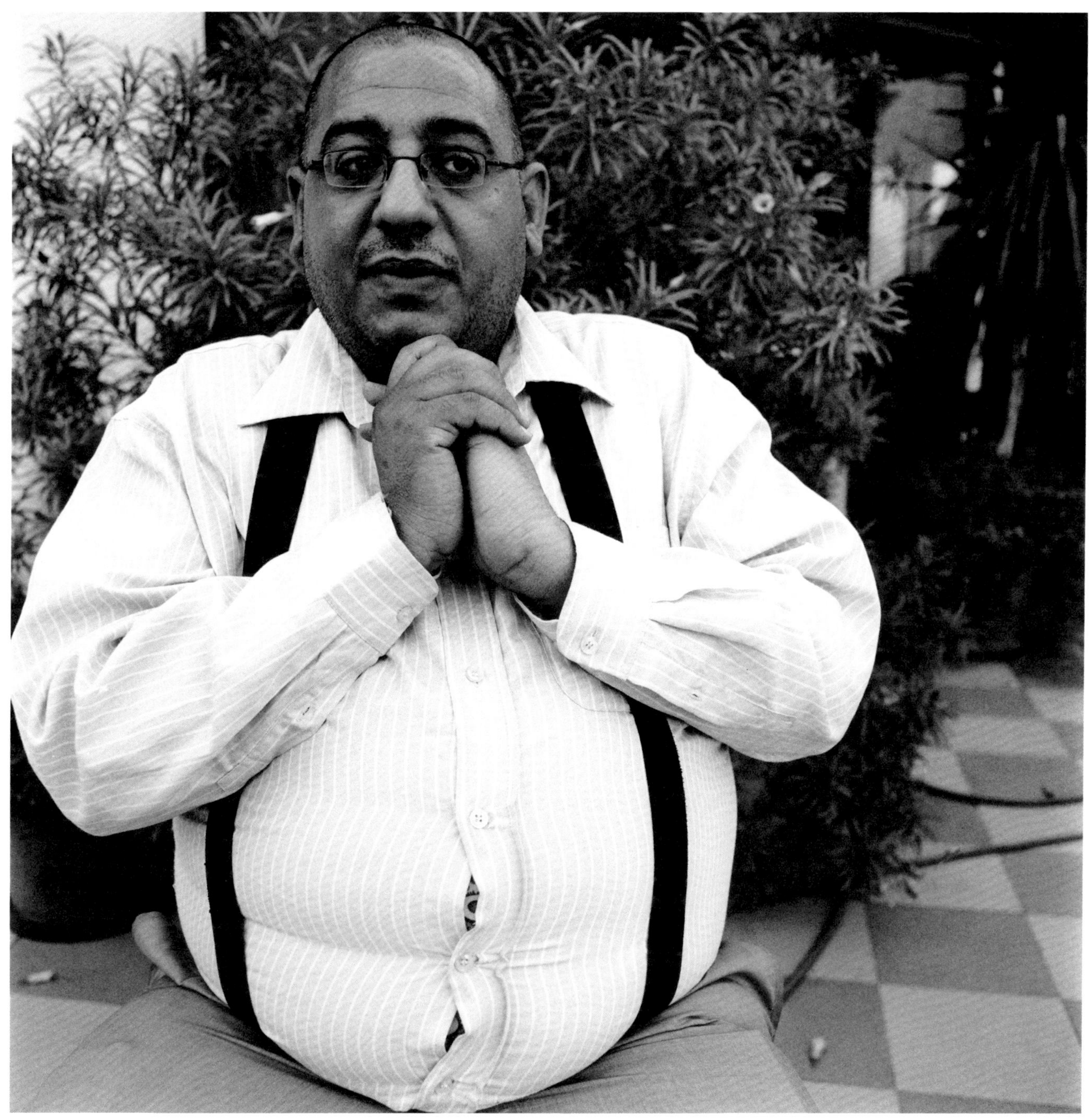

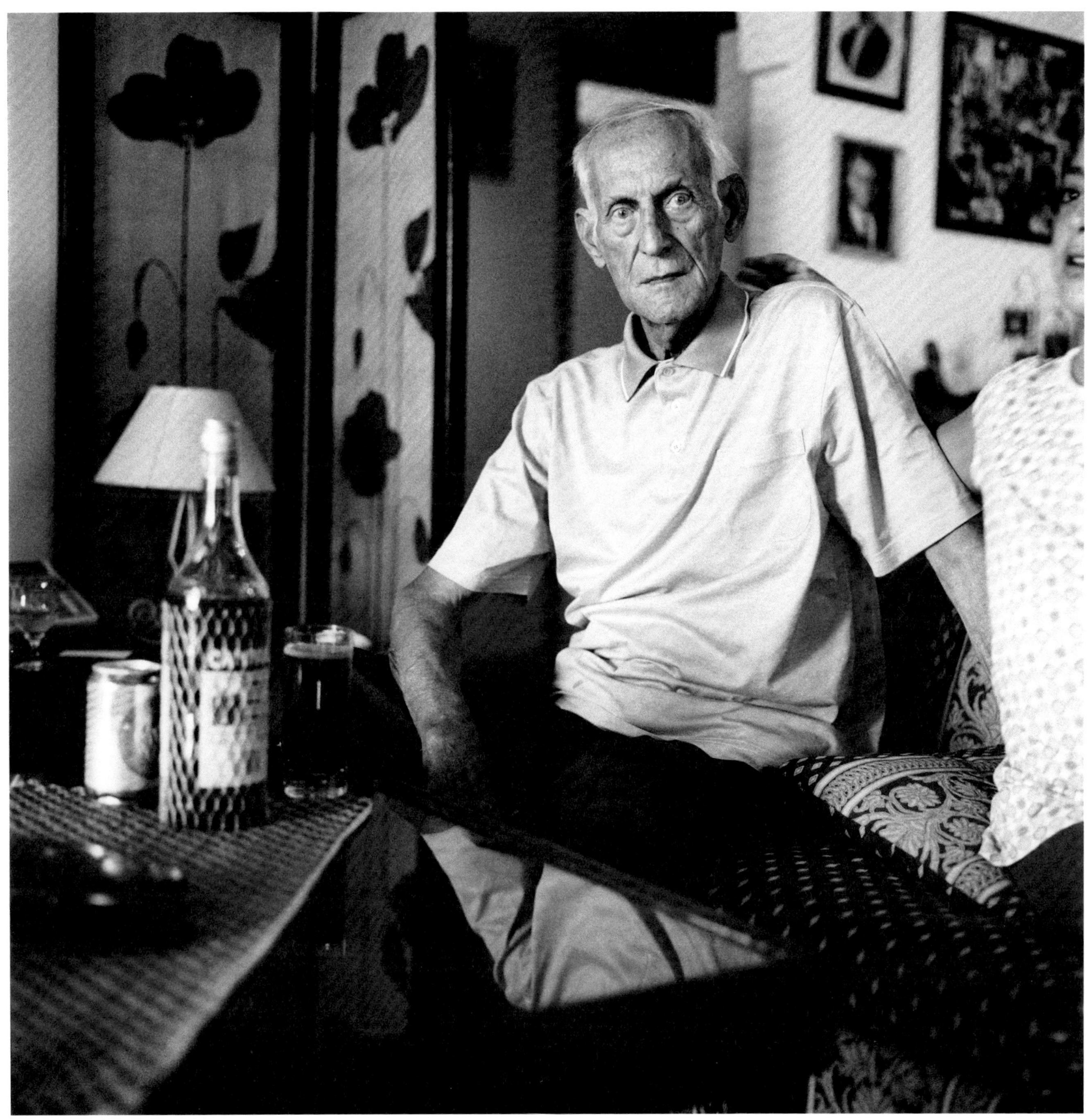

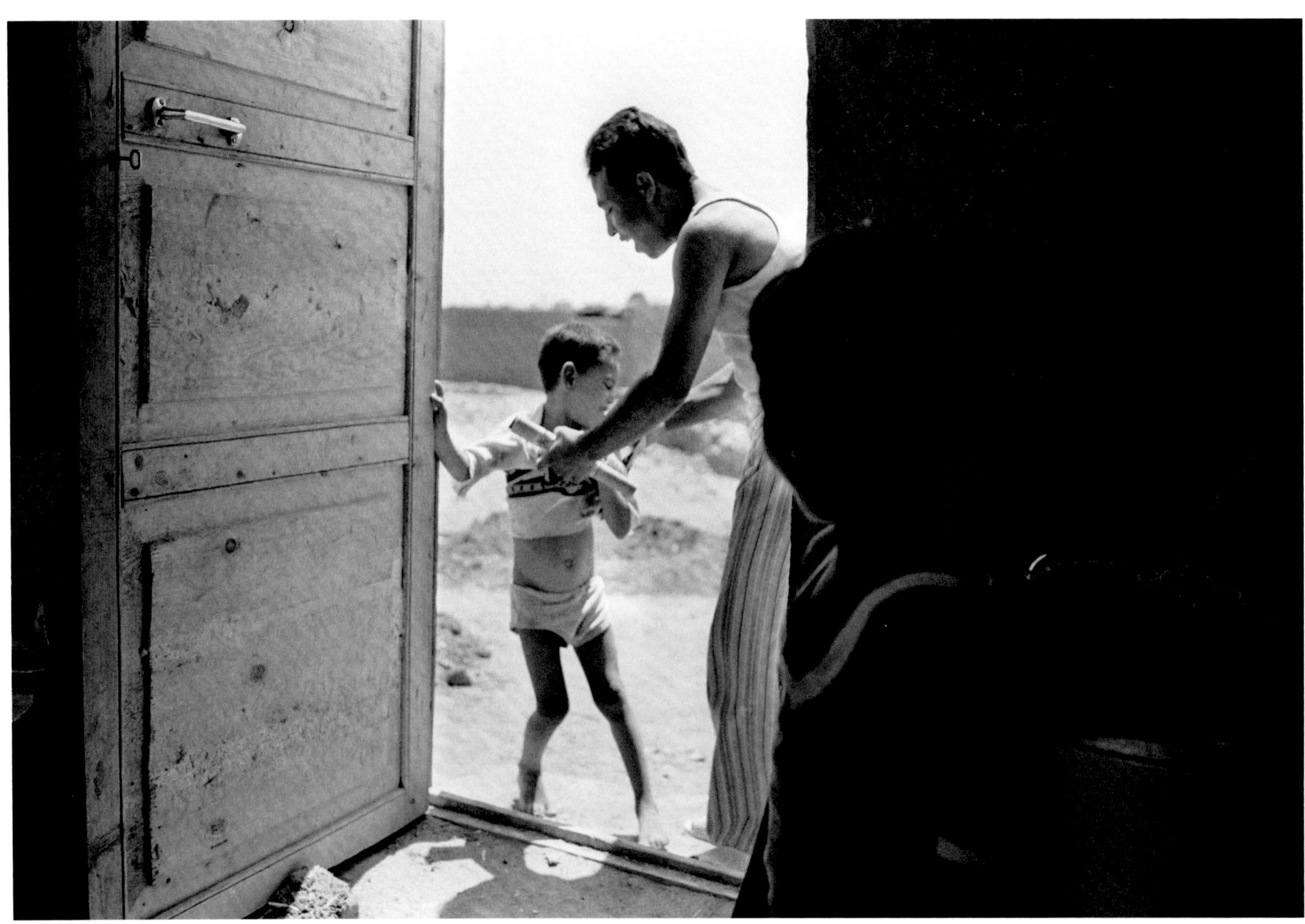

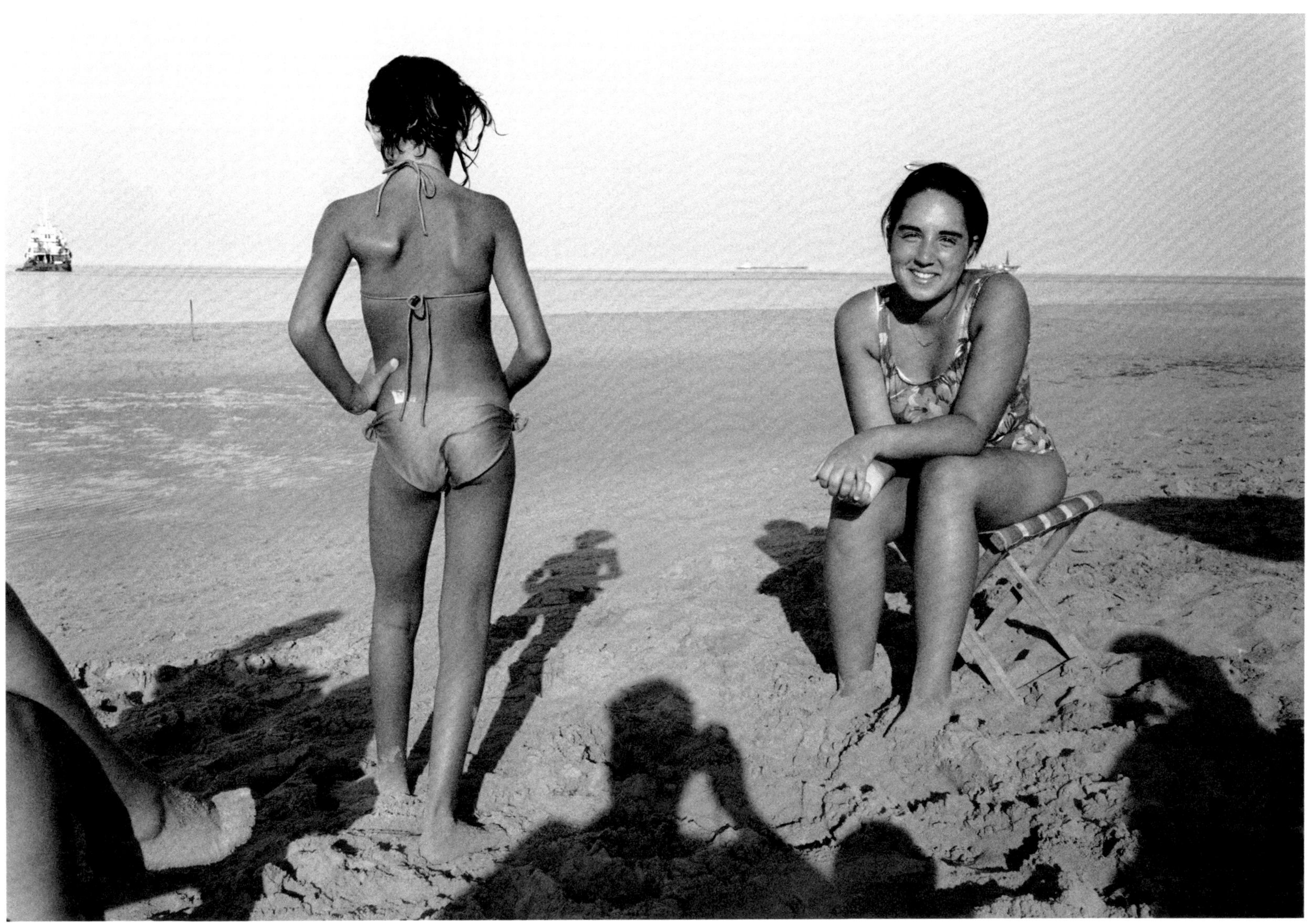

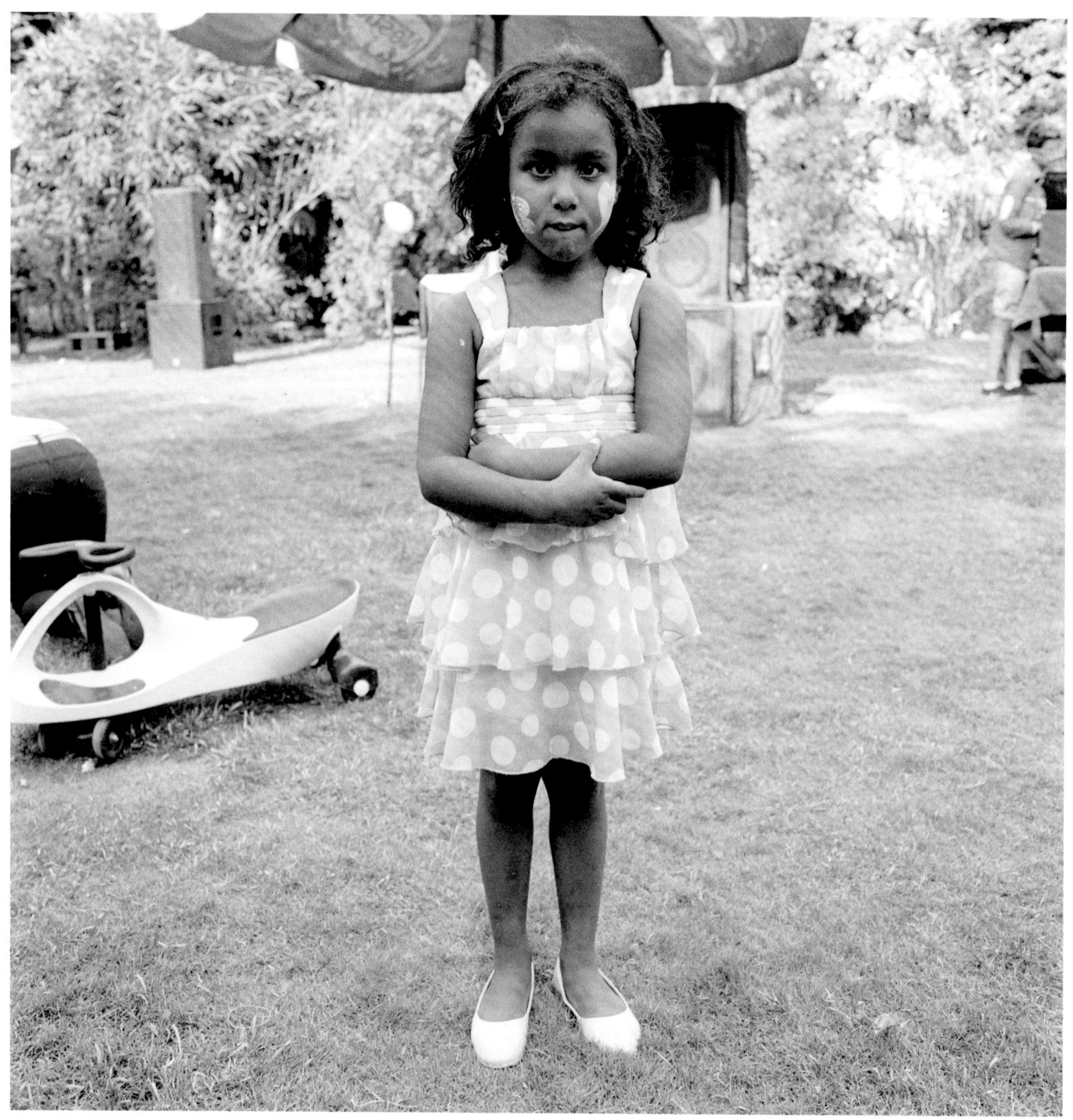

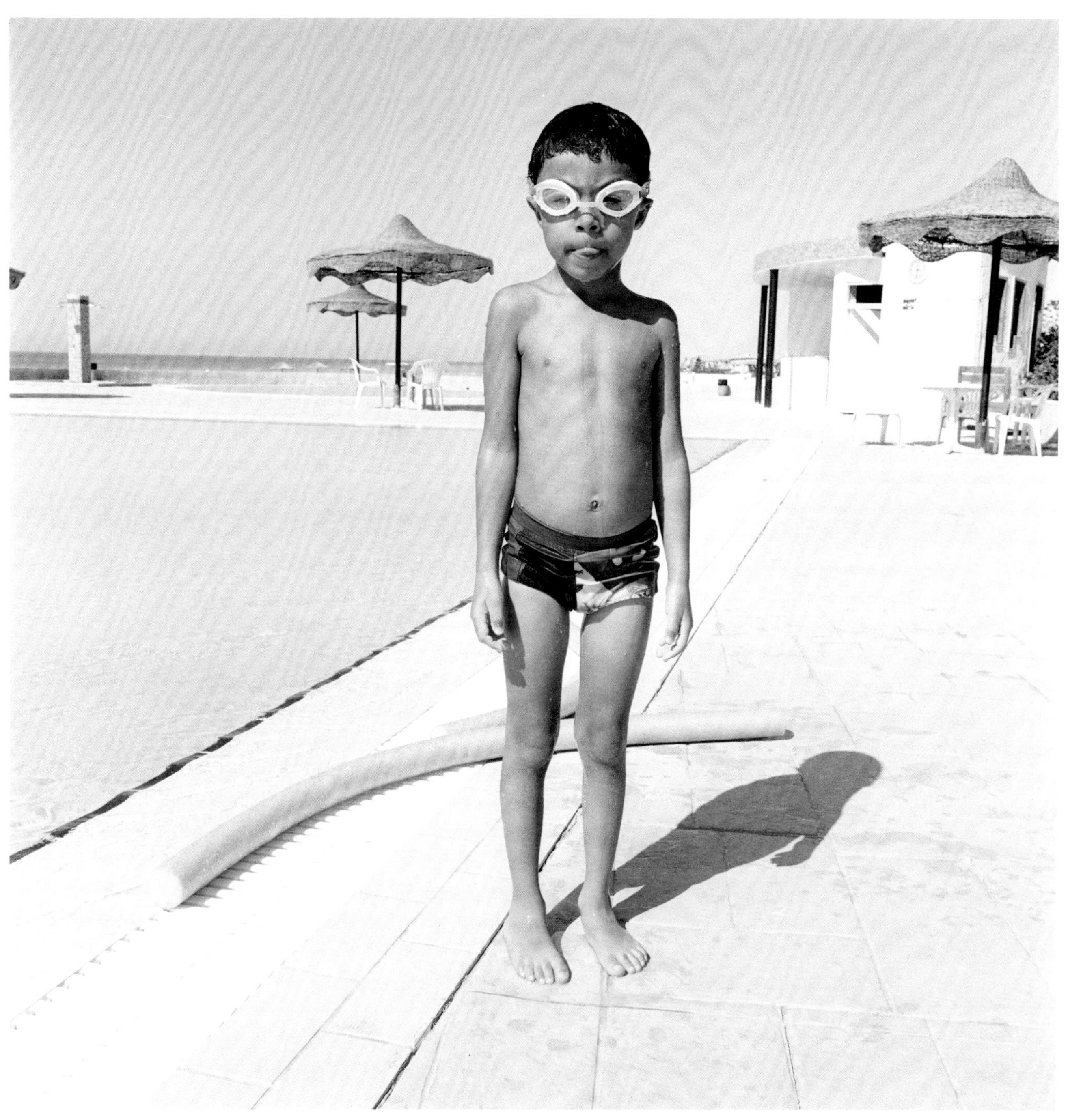

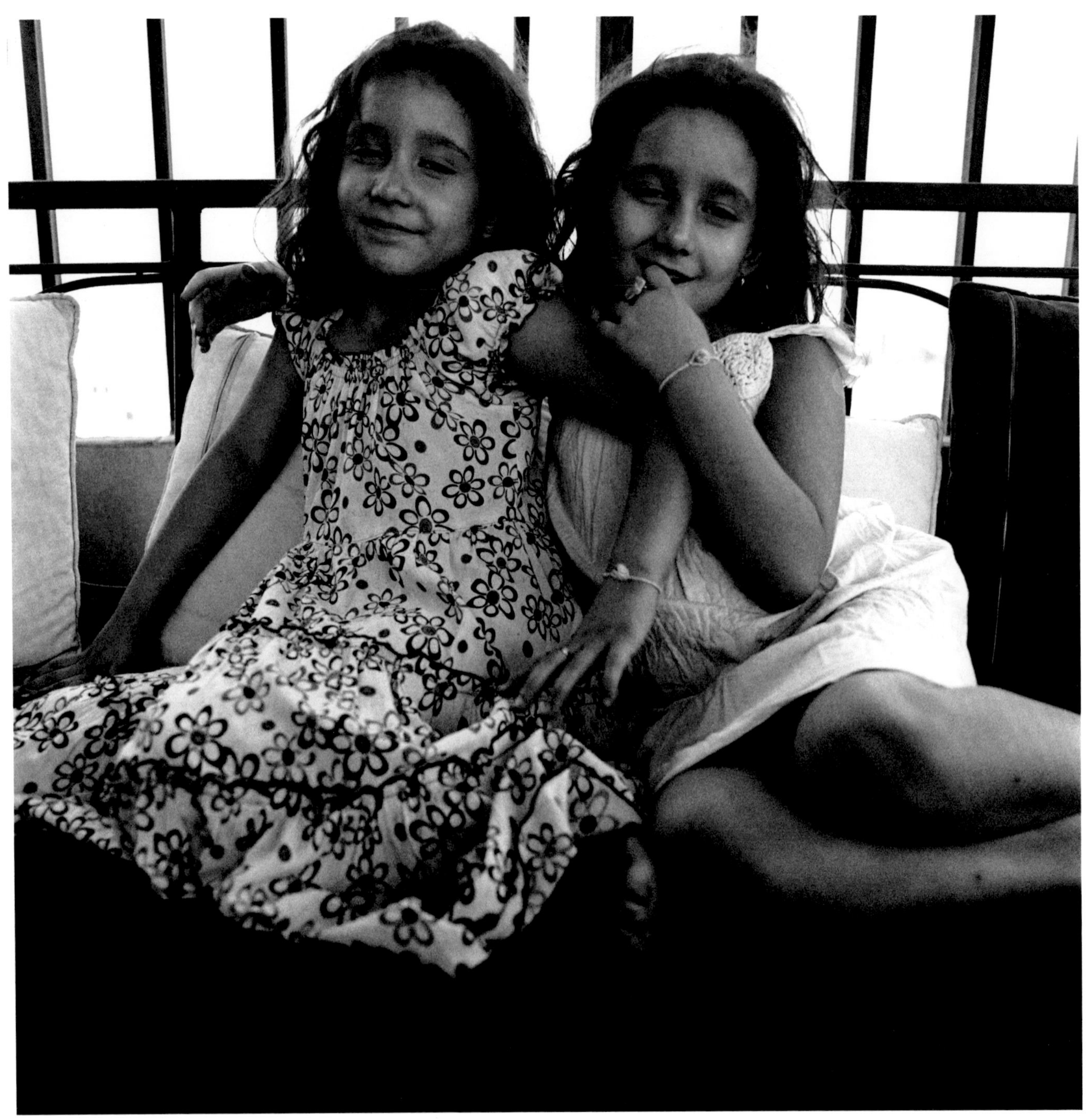

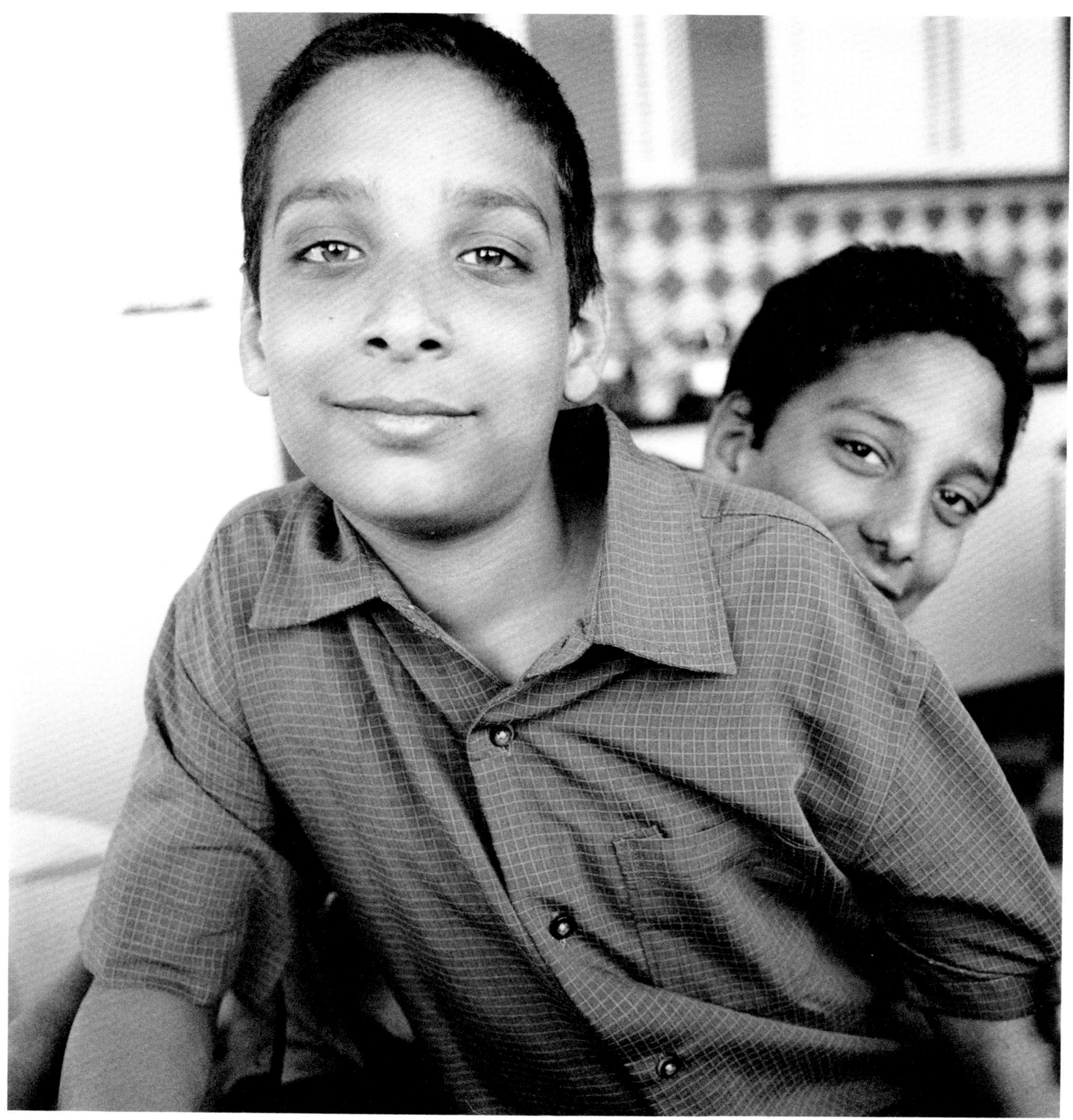

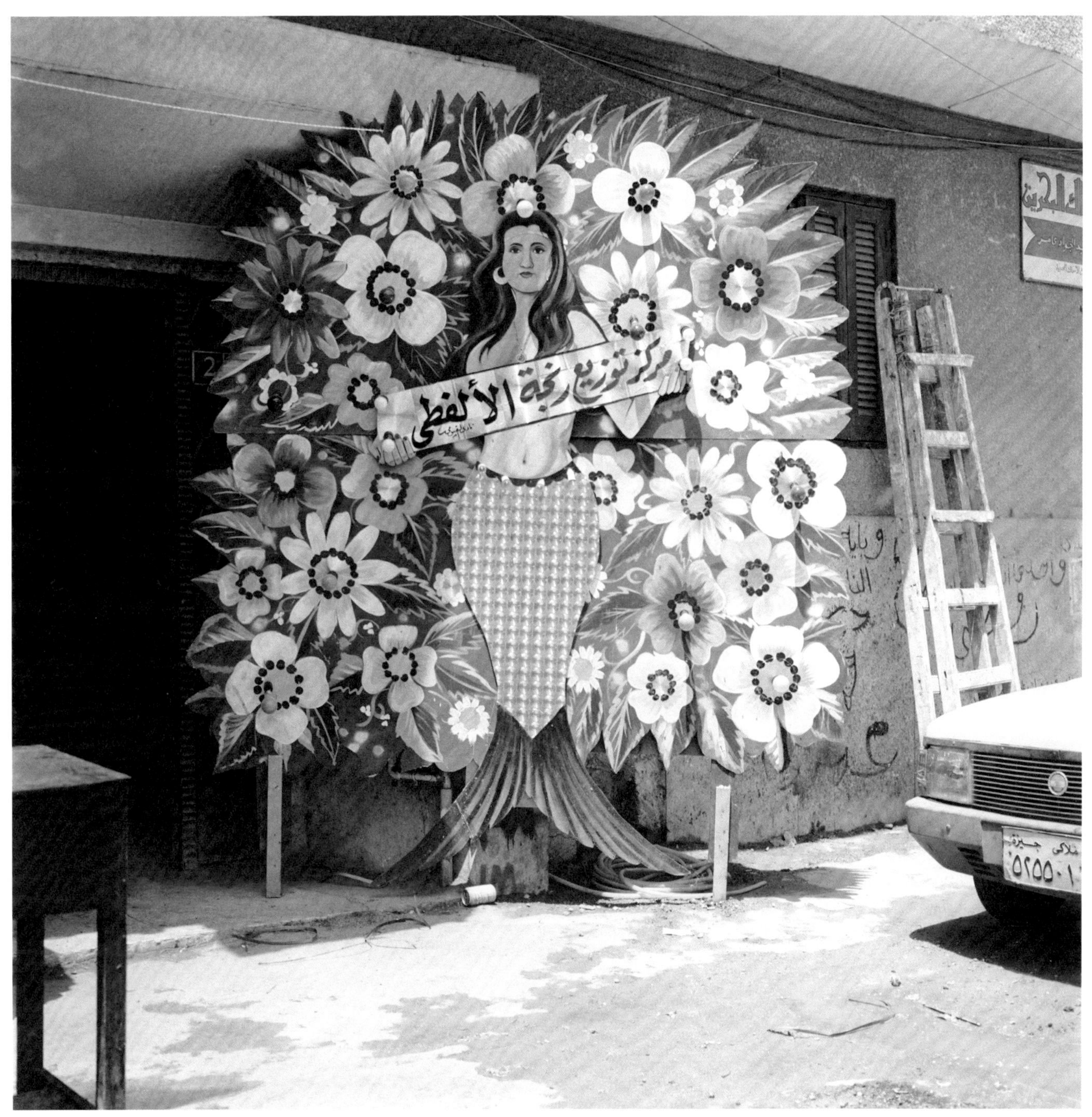

مركز توزيع دجة الألفطى

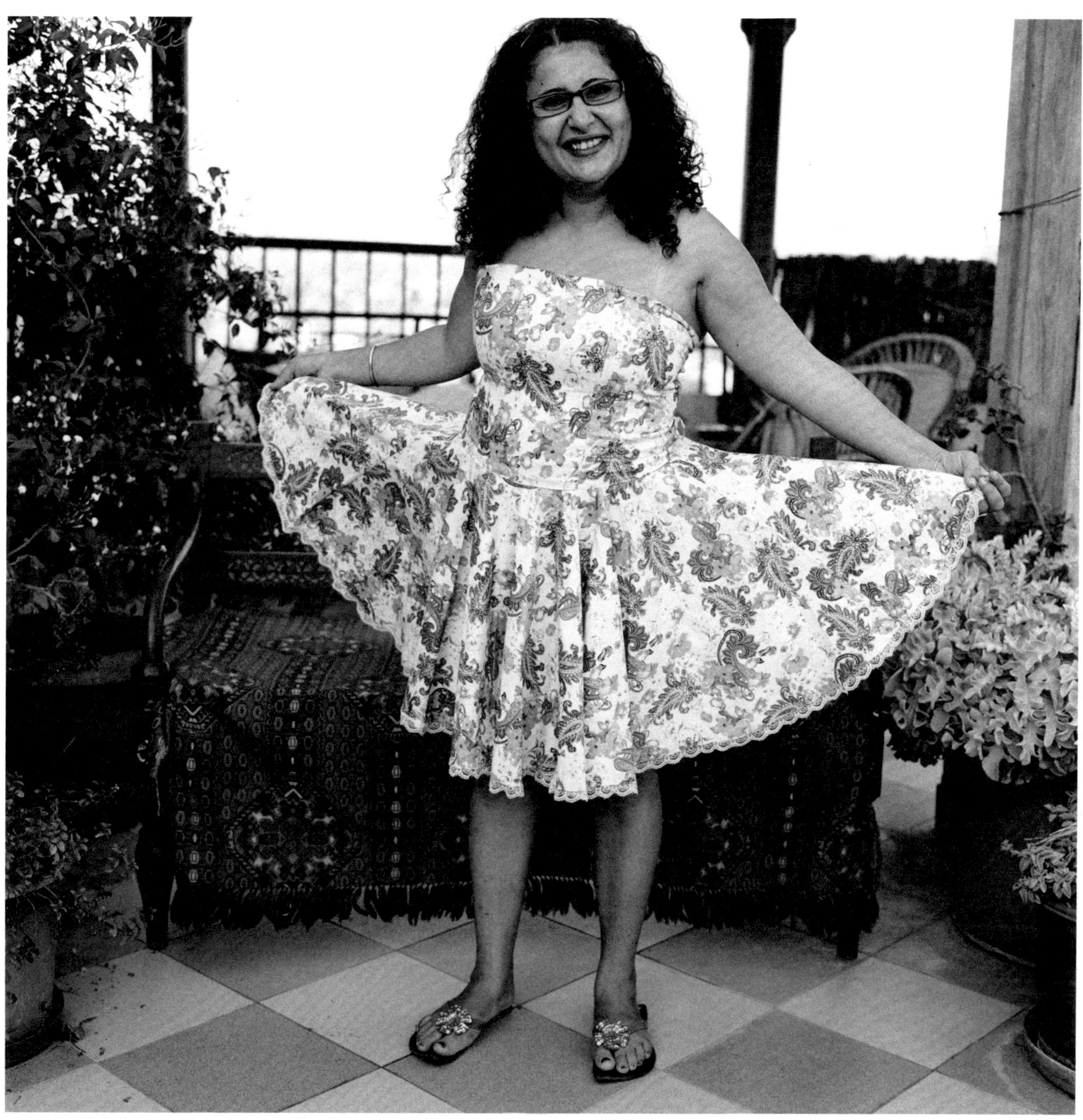

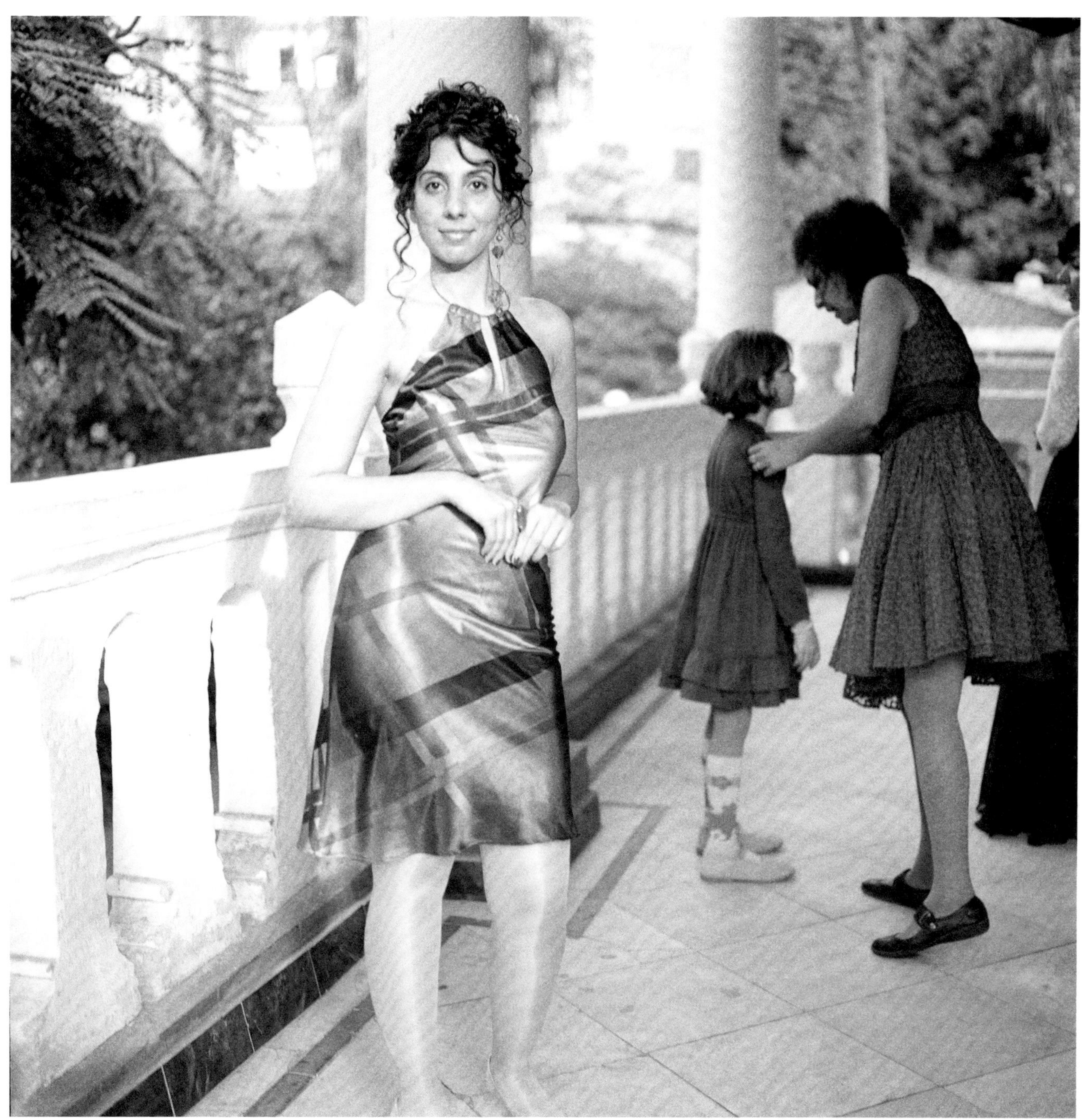

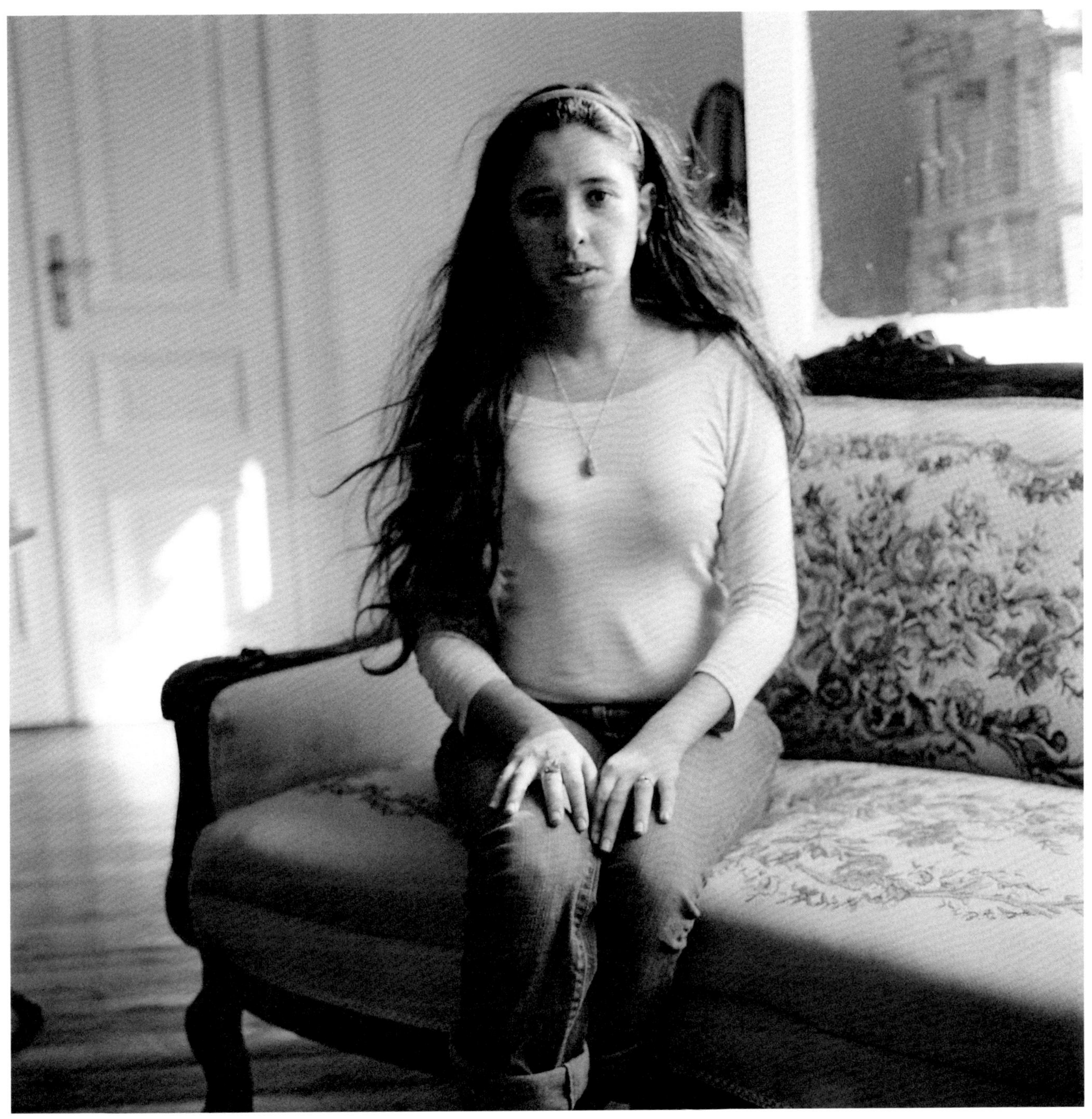

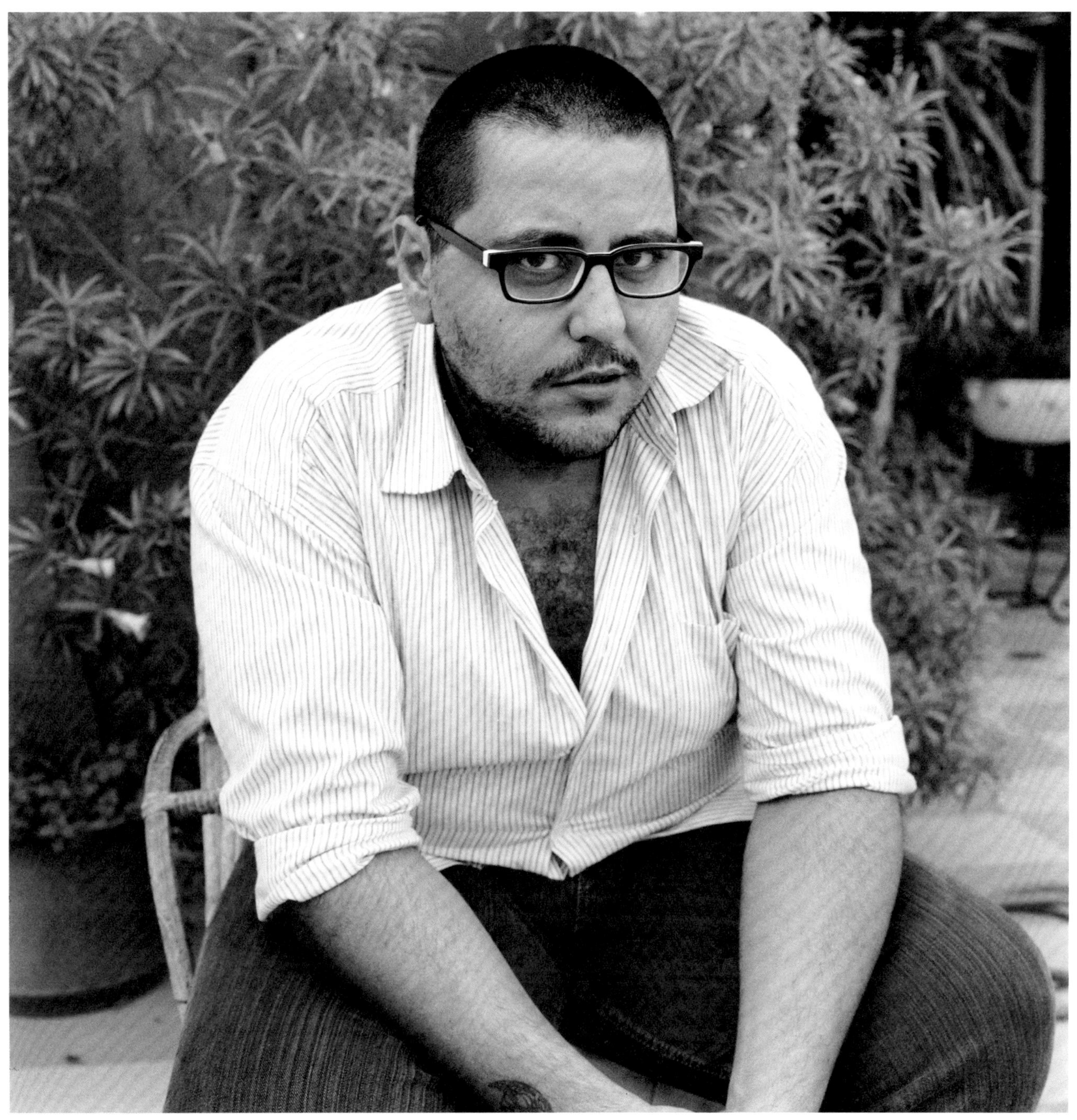

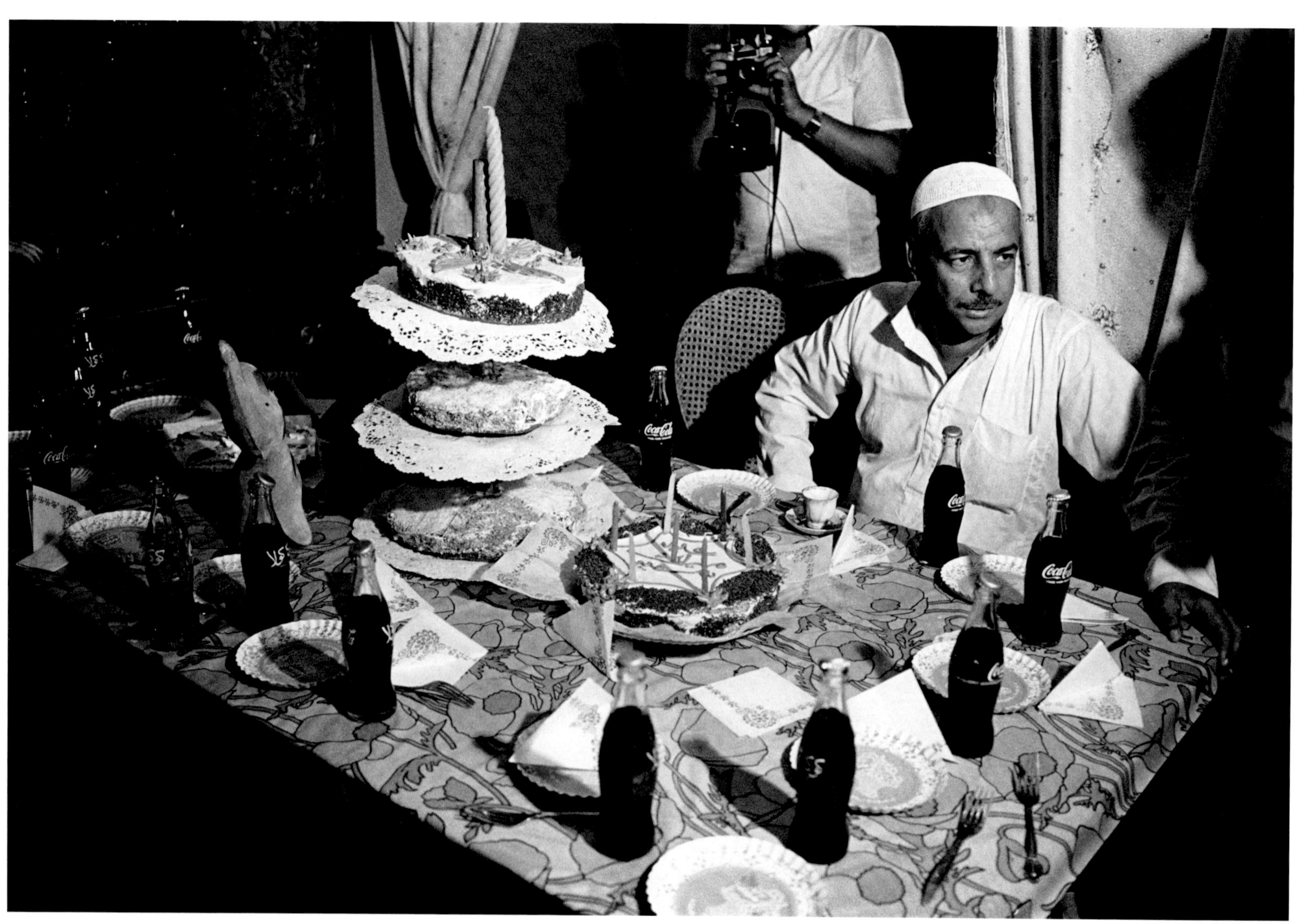

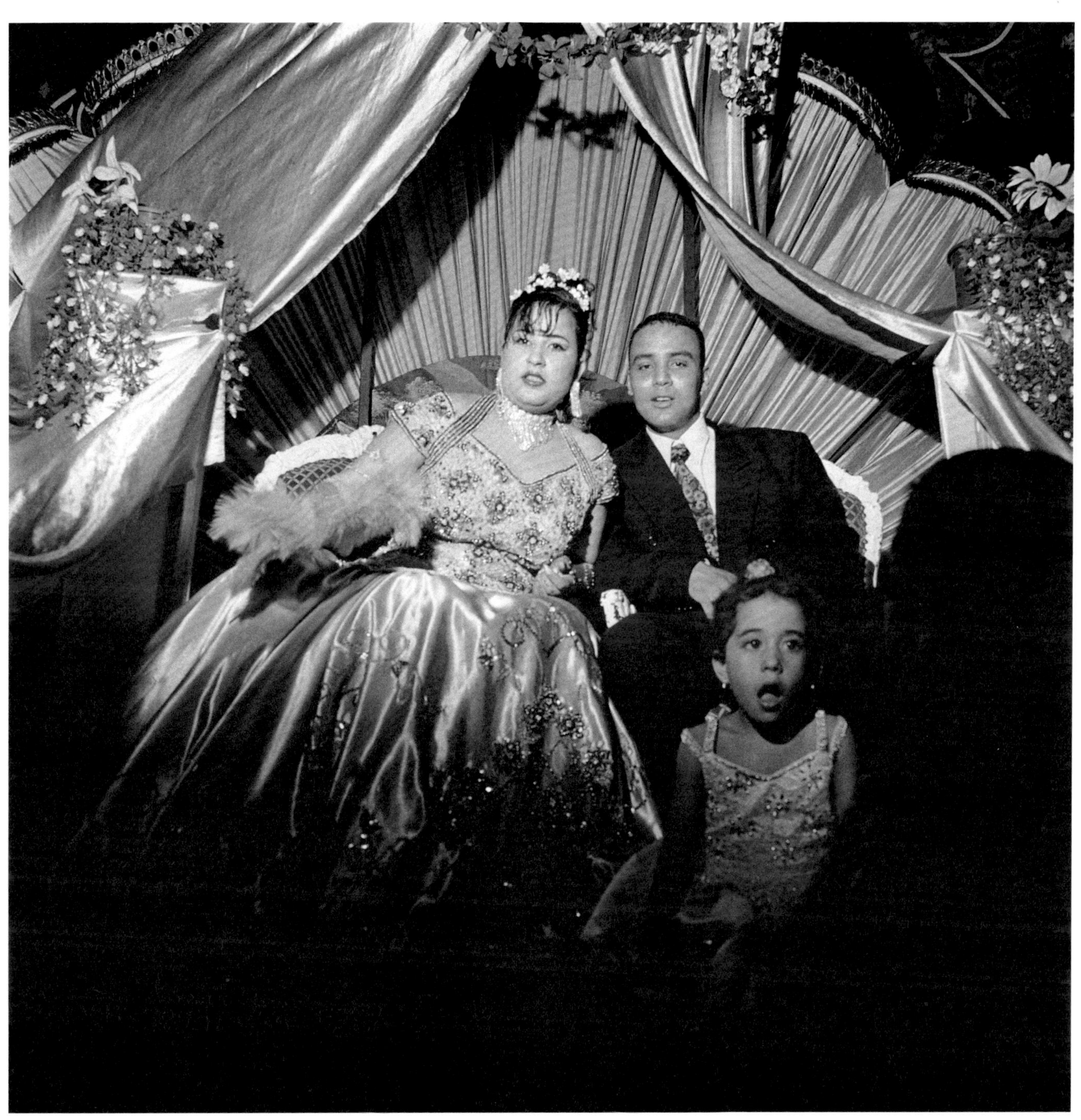

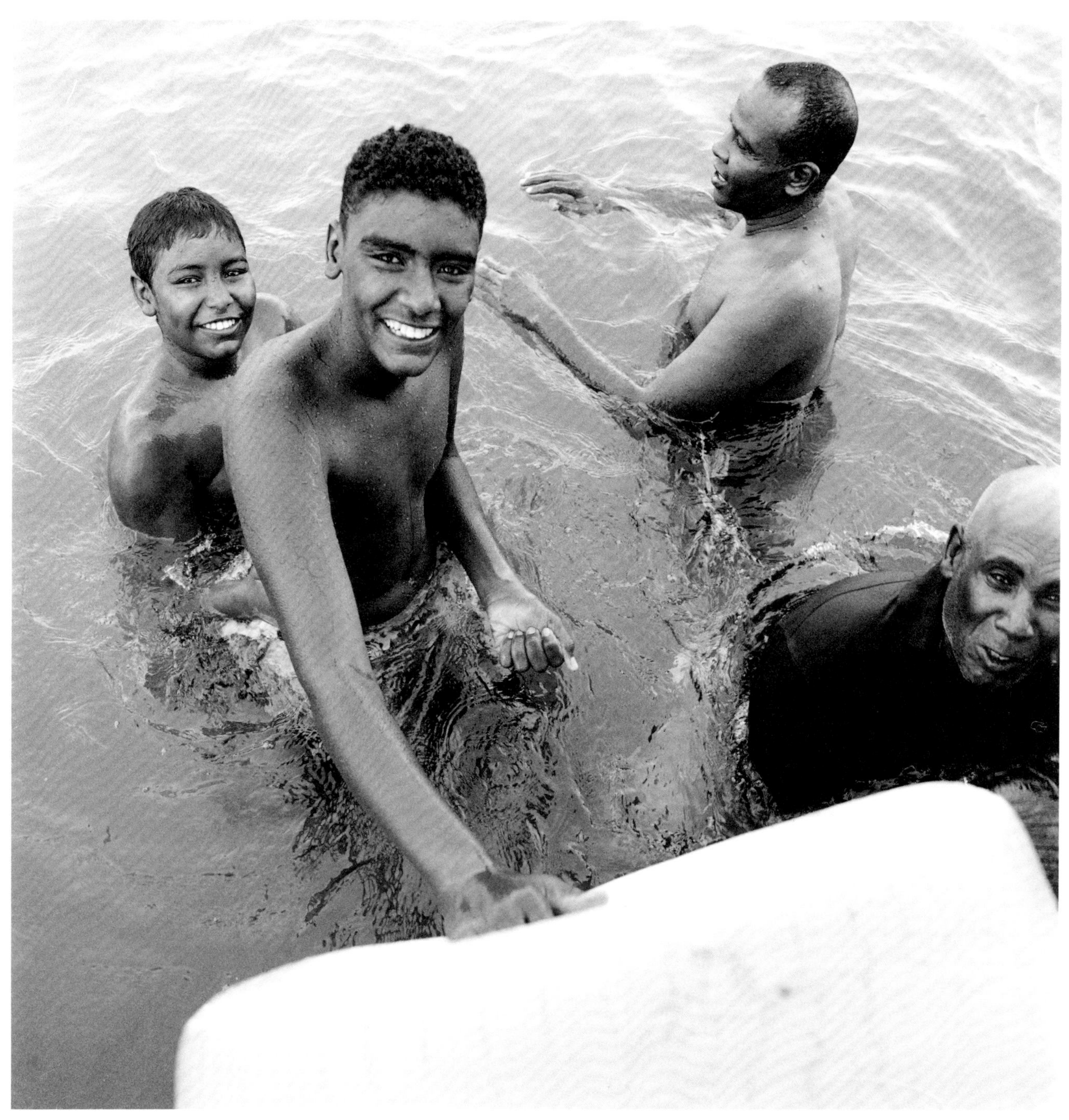

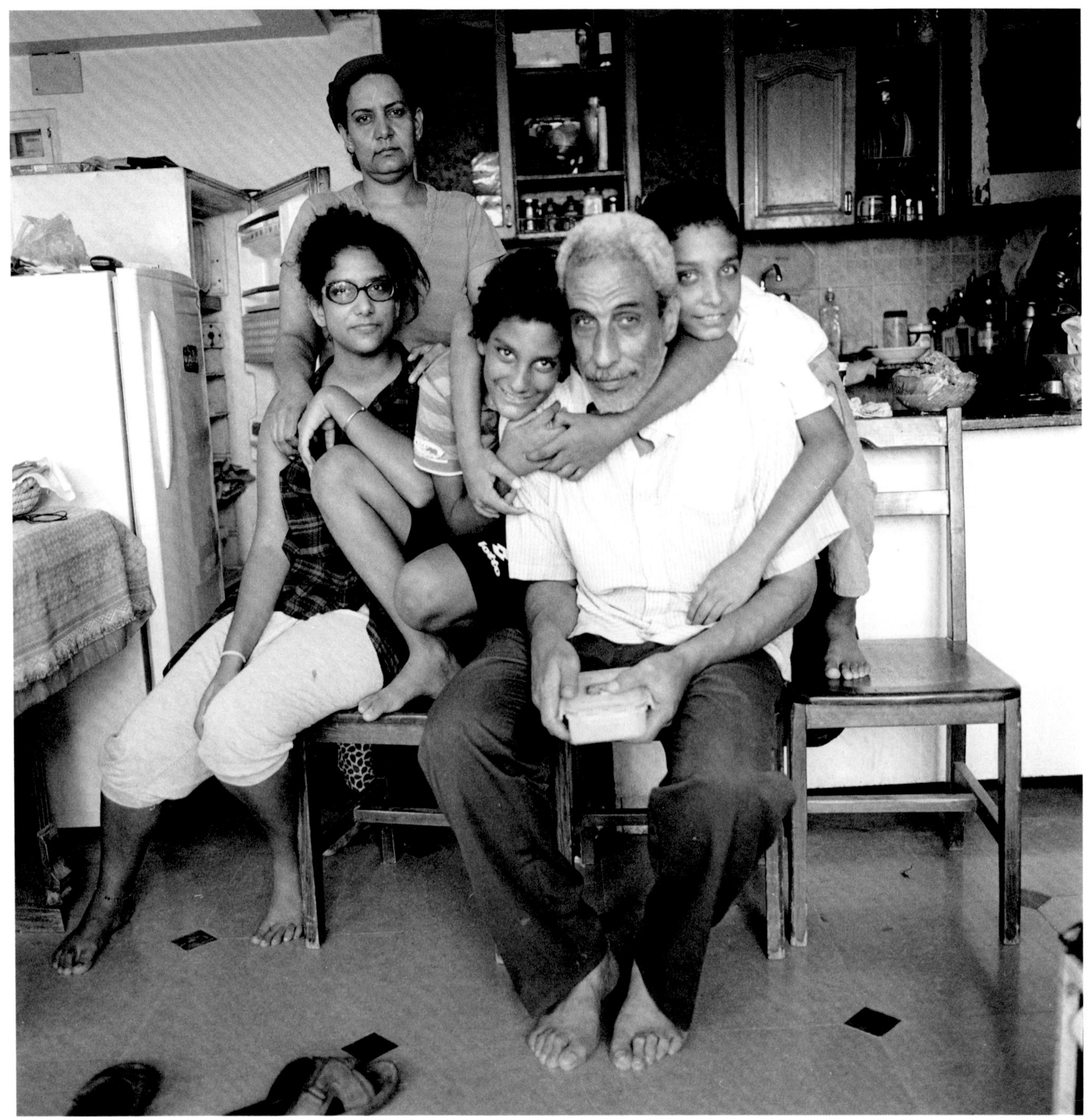

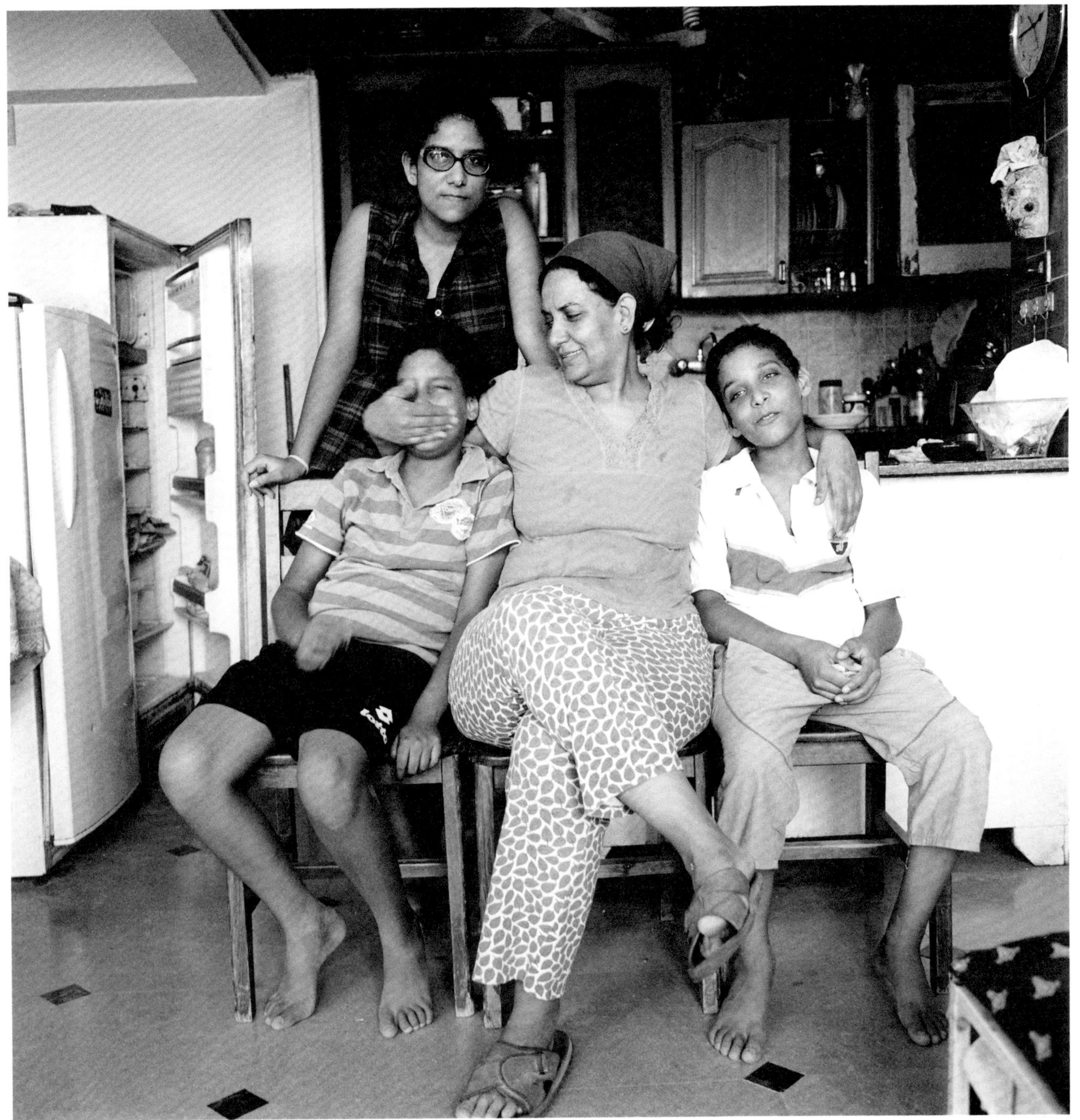

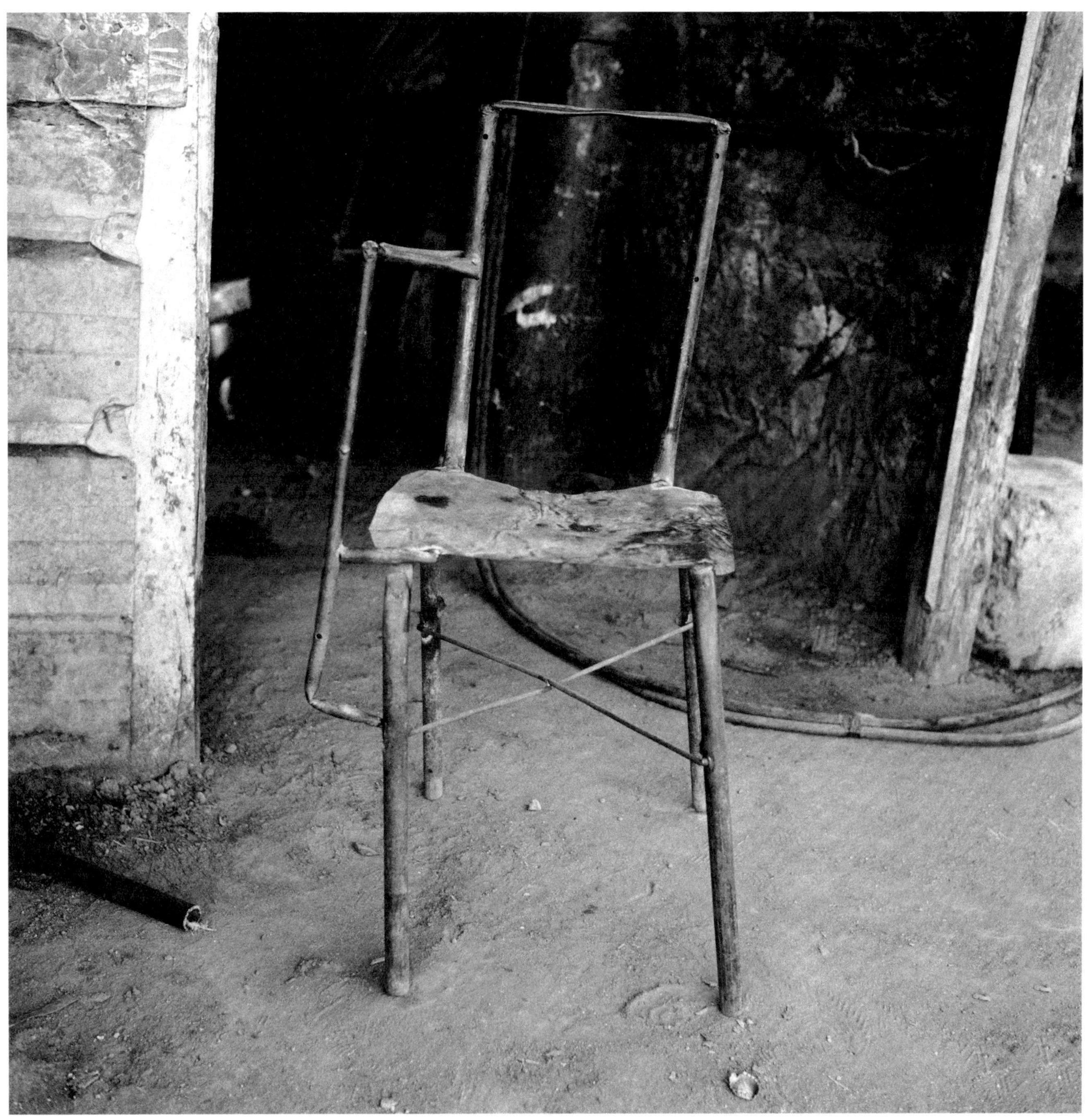

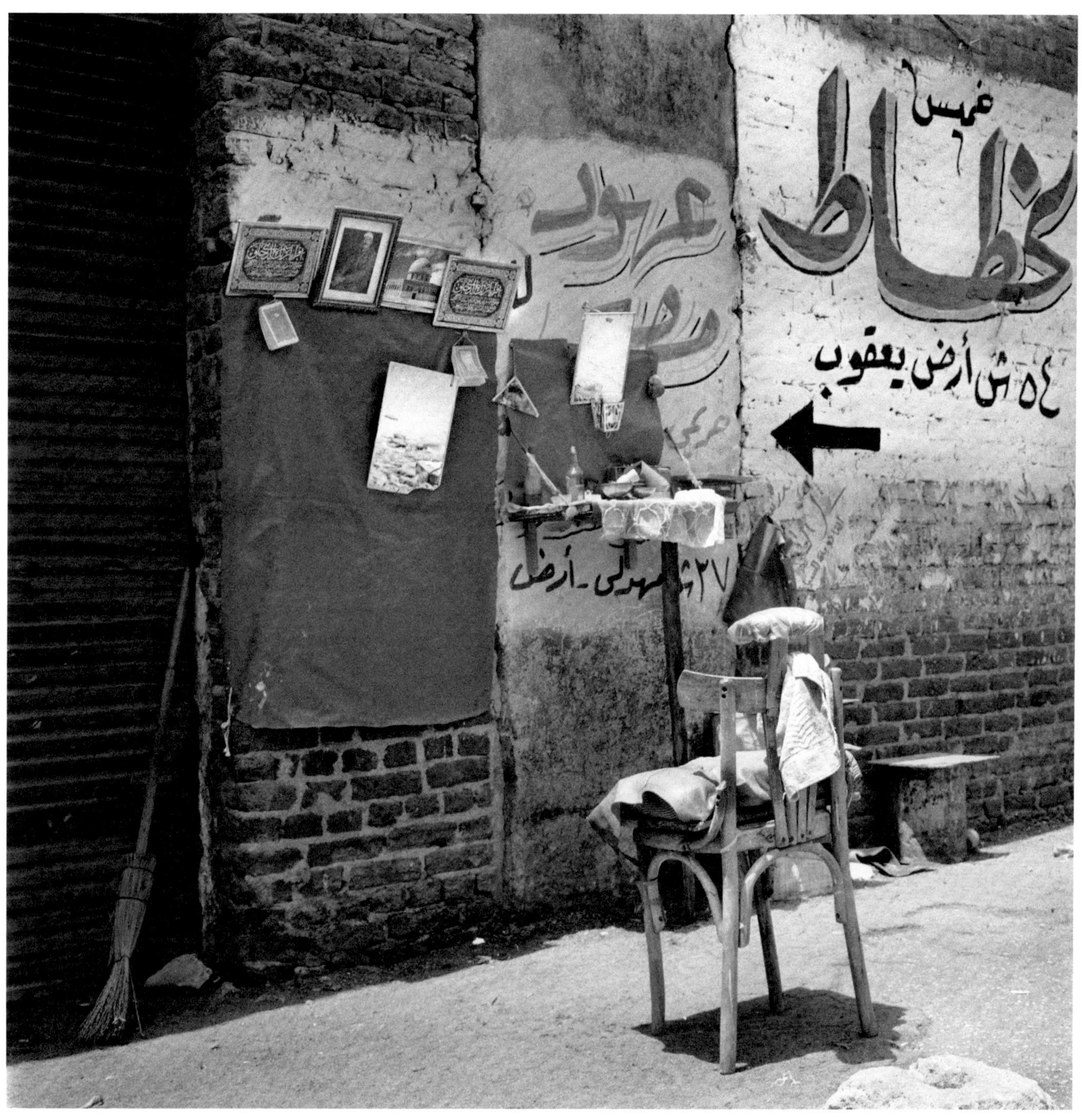

٥٤ ش أرض يعقوب

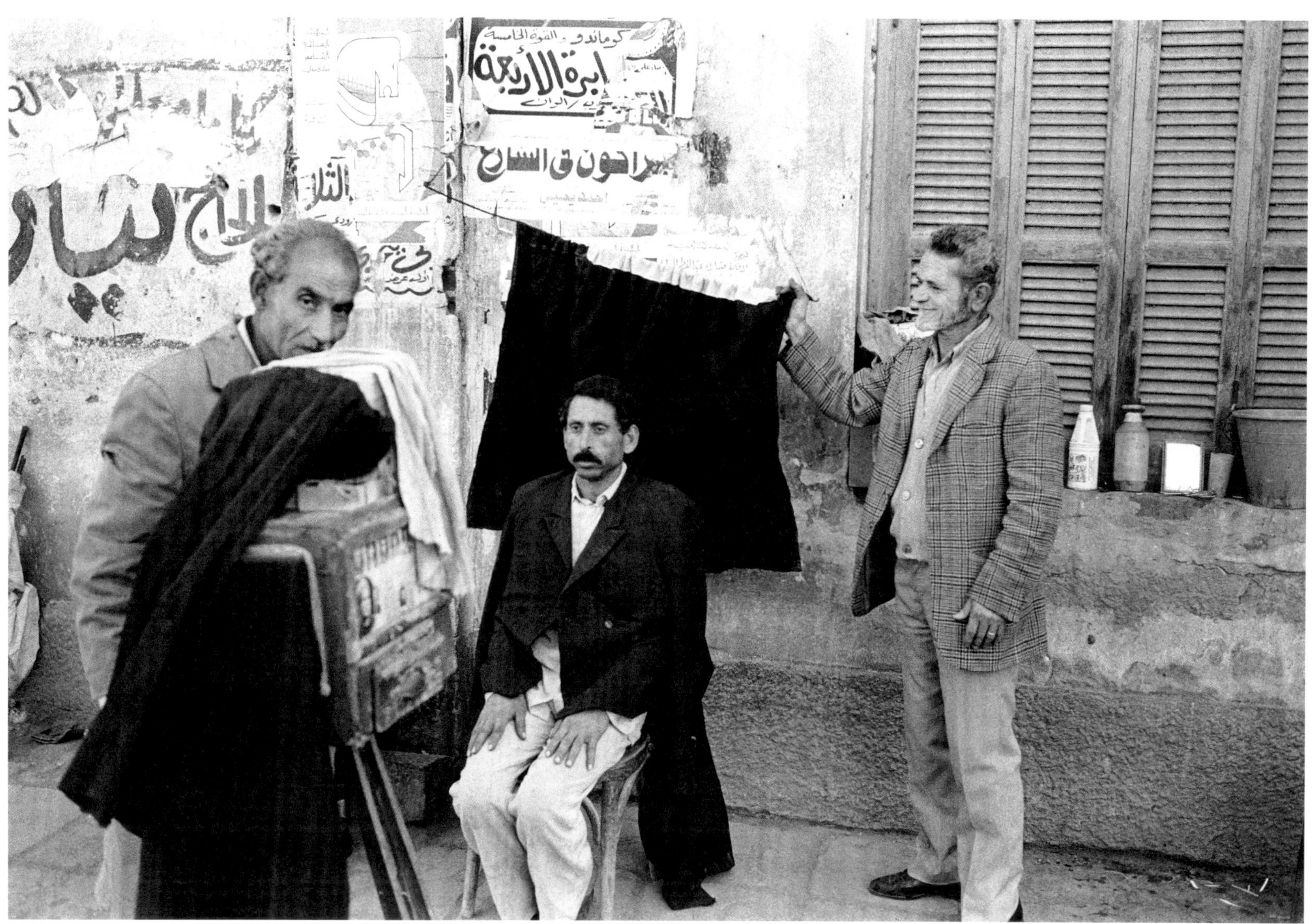
كوماندو ـ القوة الخامسة
ابرة الاربعة
يراهون فى السلاح
الثلا
الحاج تيار

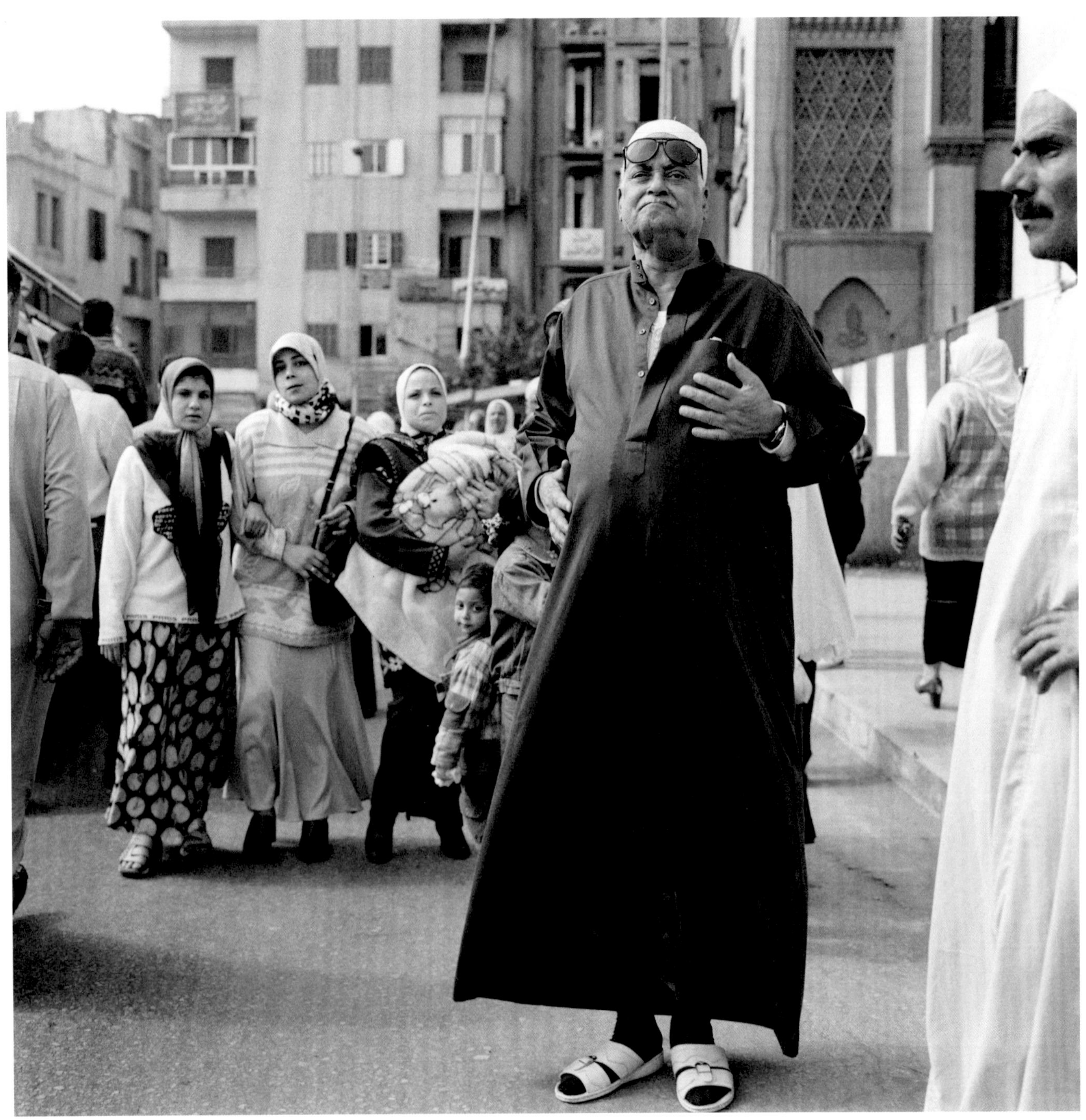

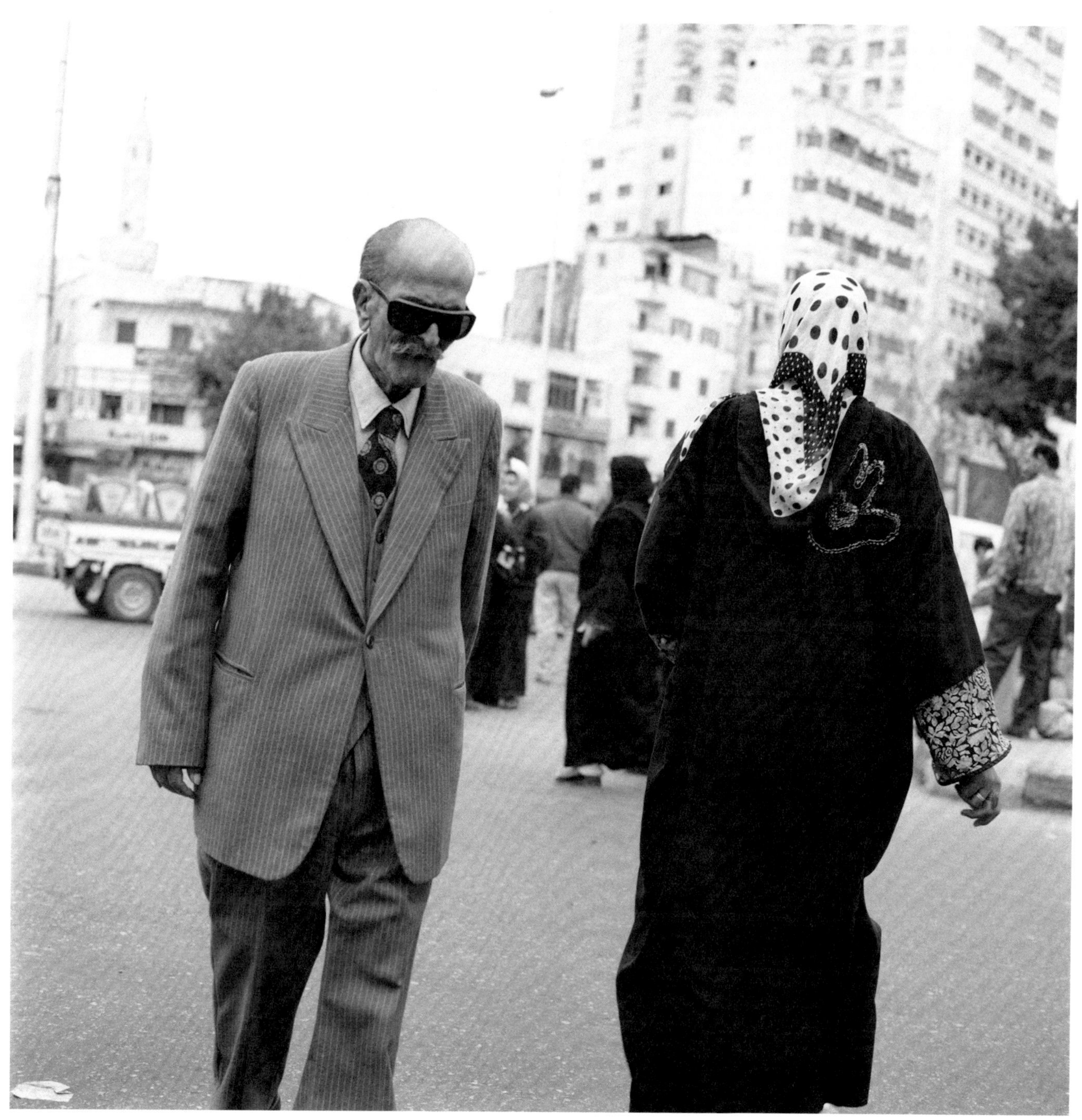

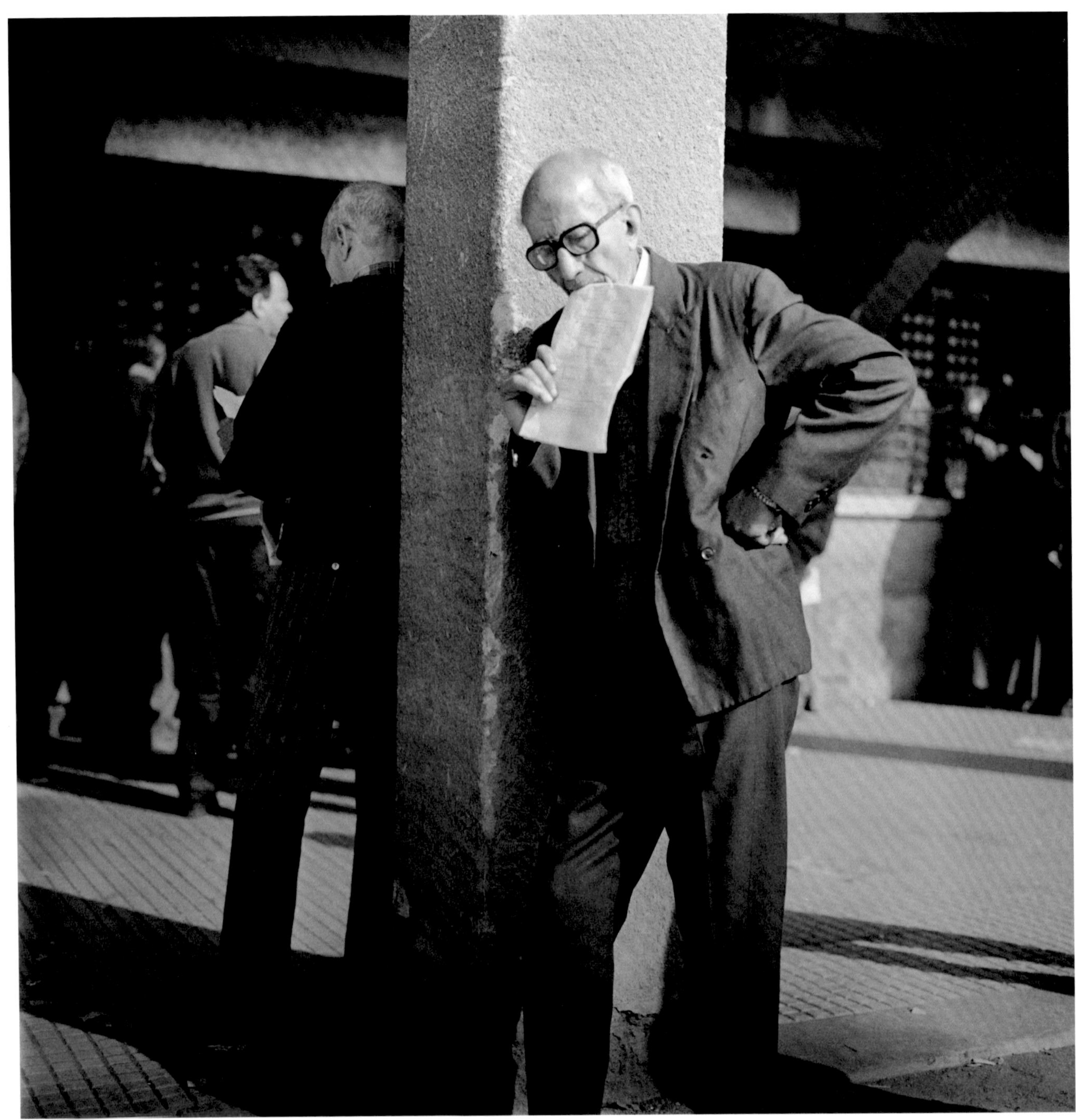

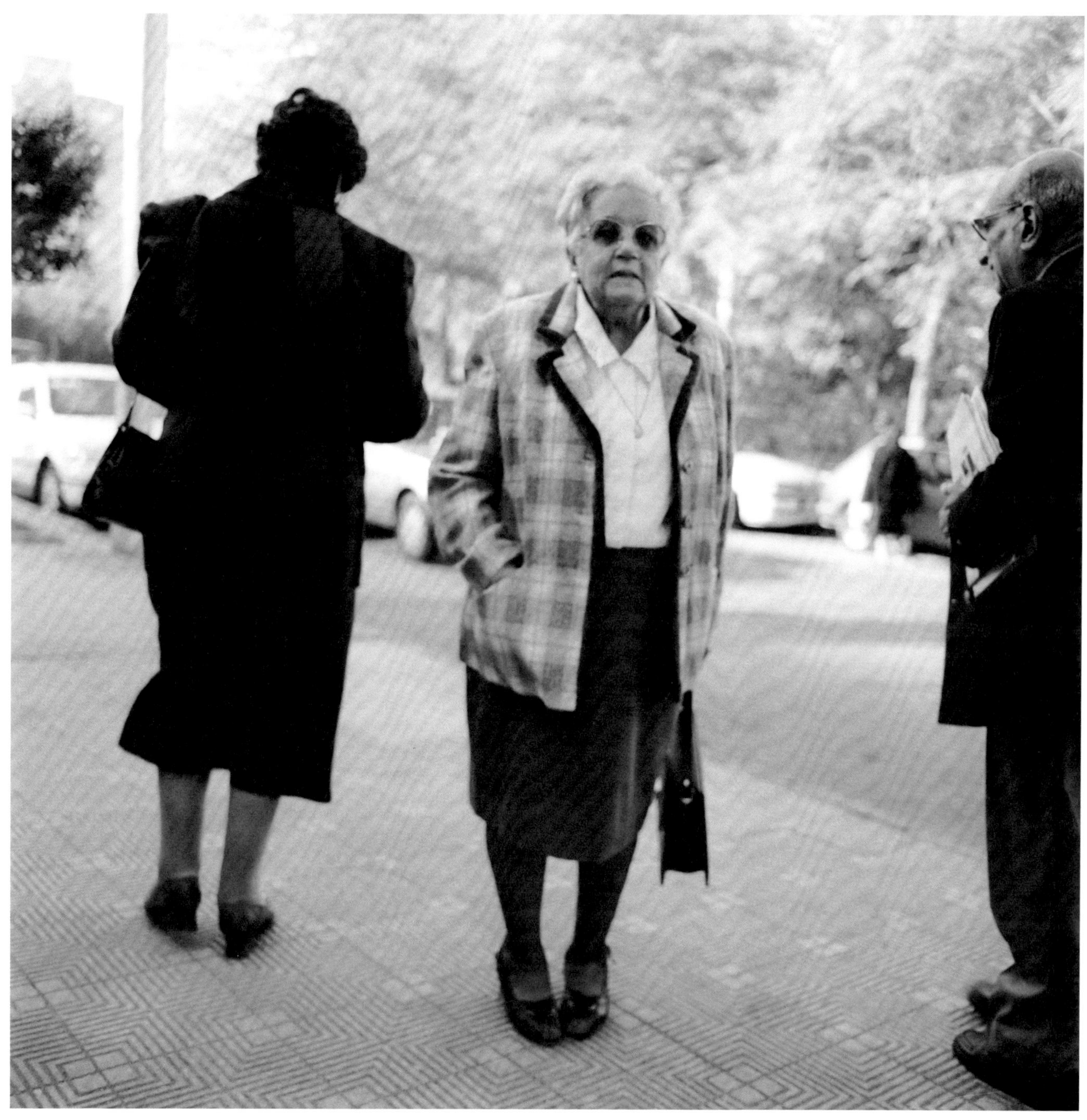

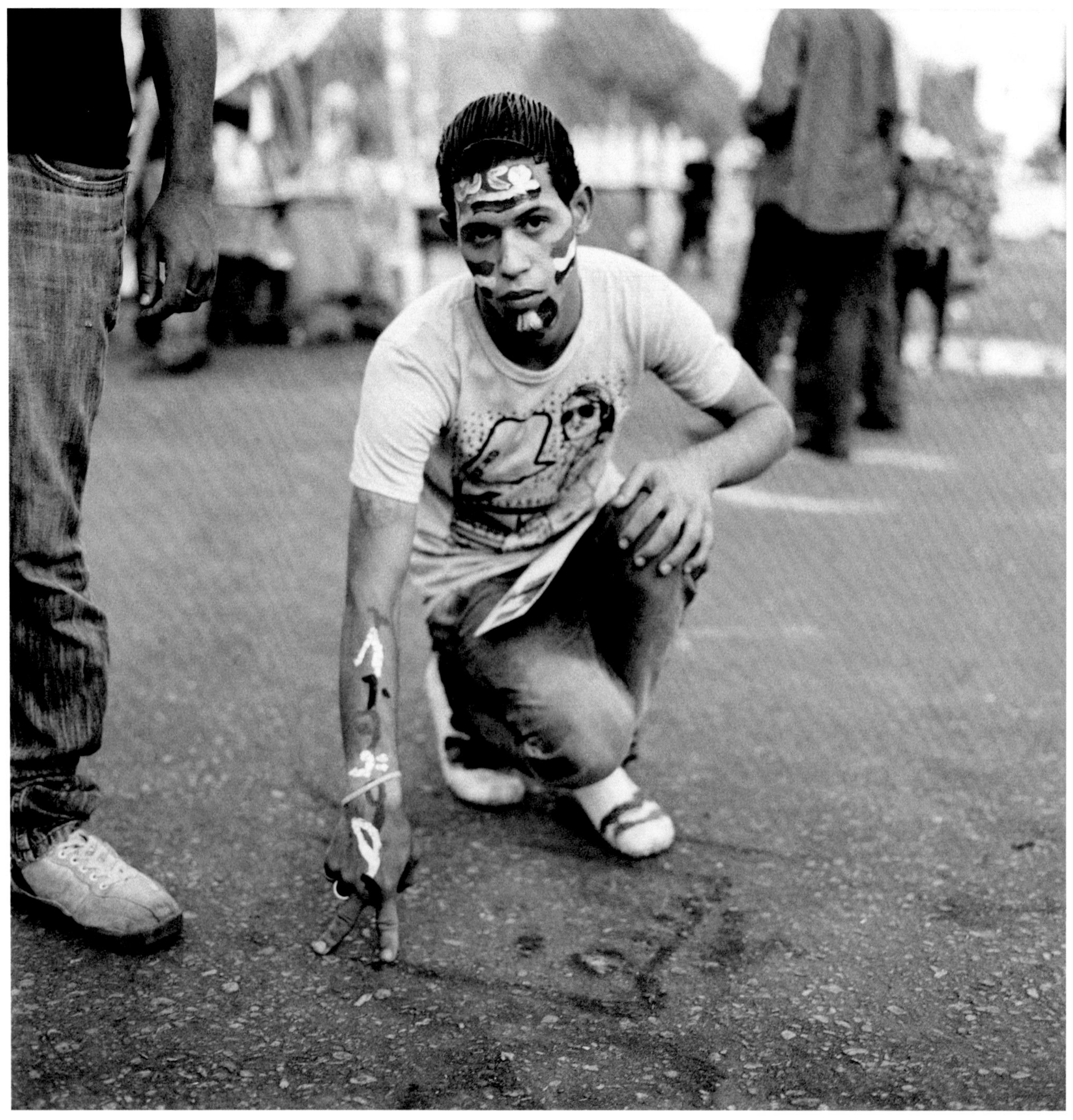

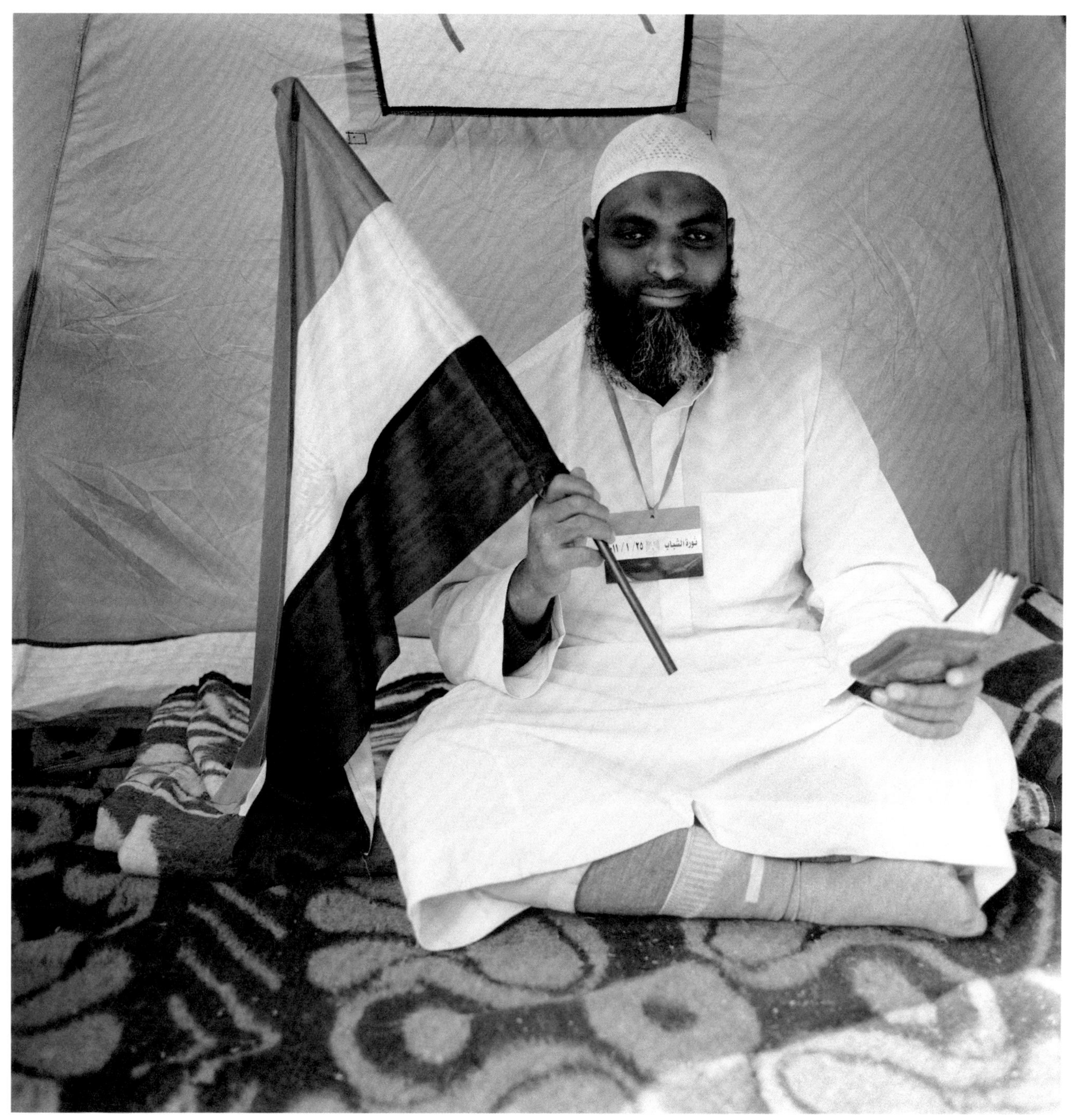

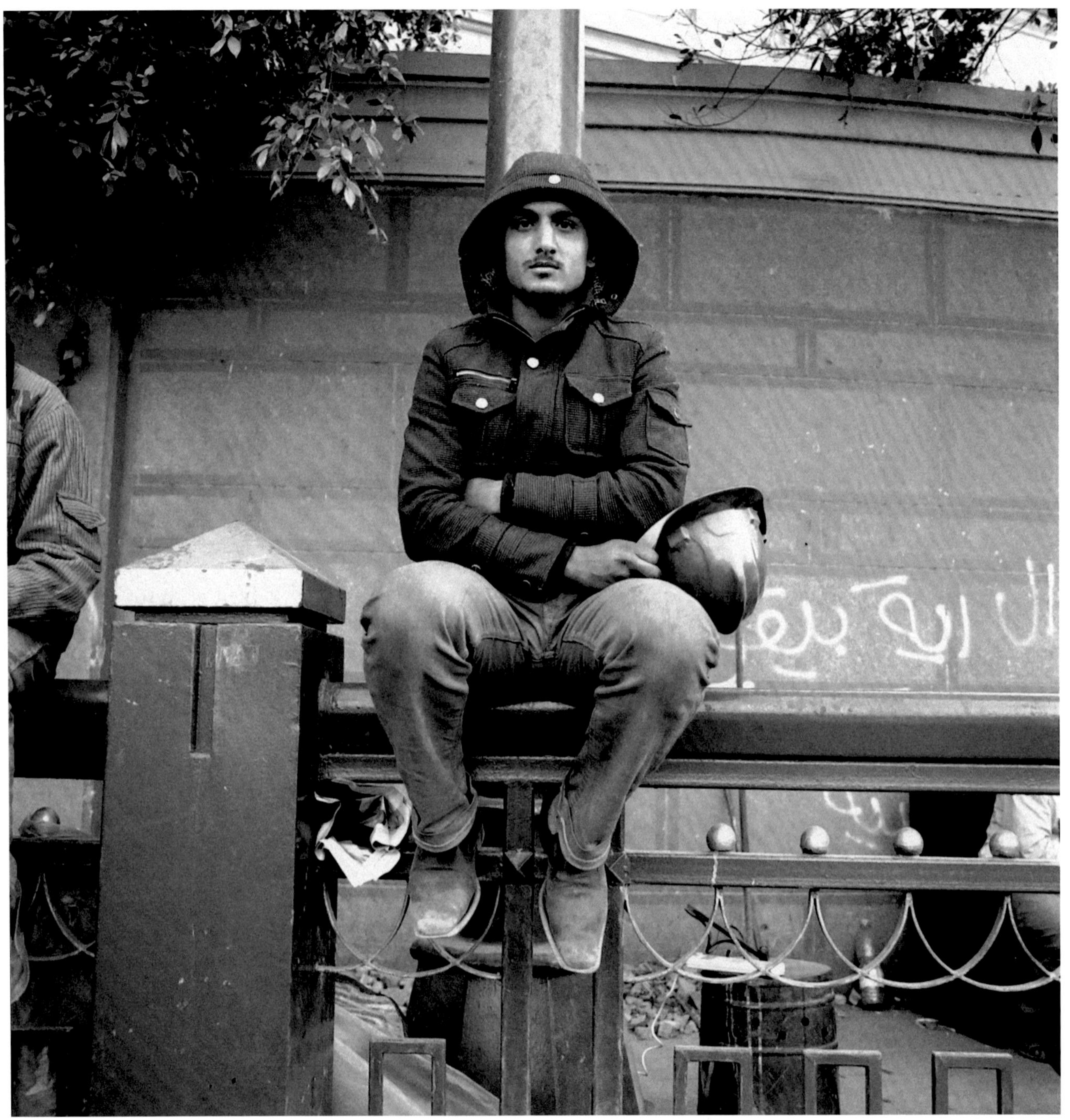

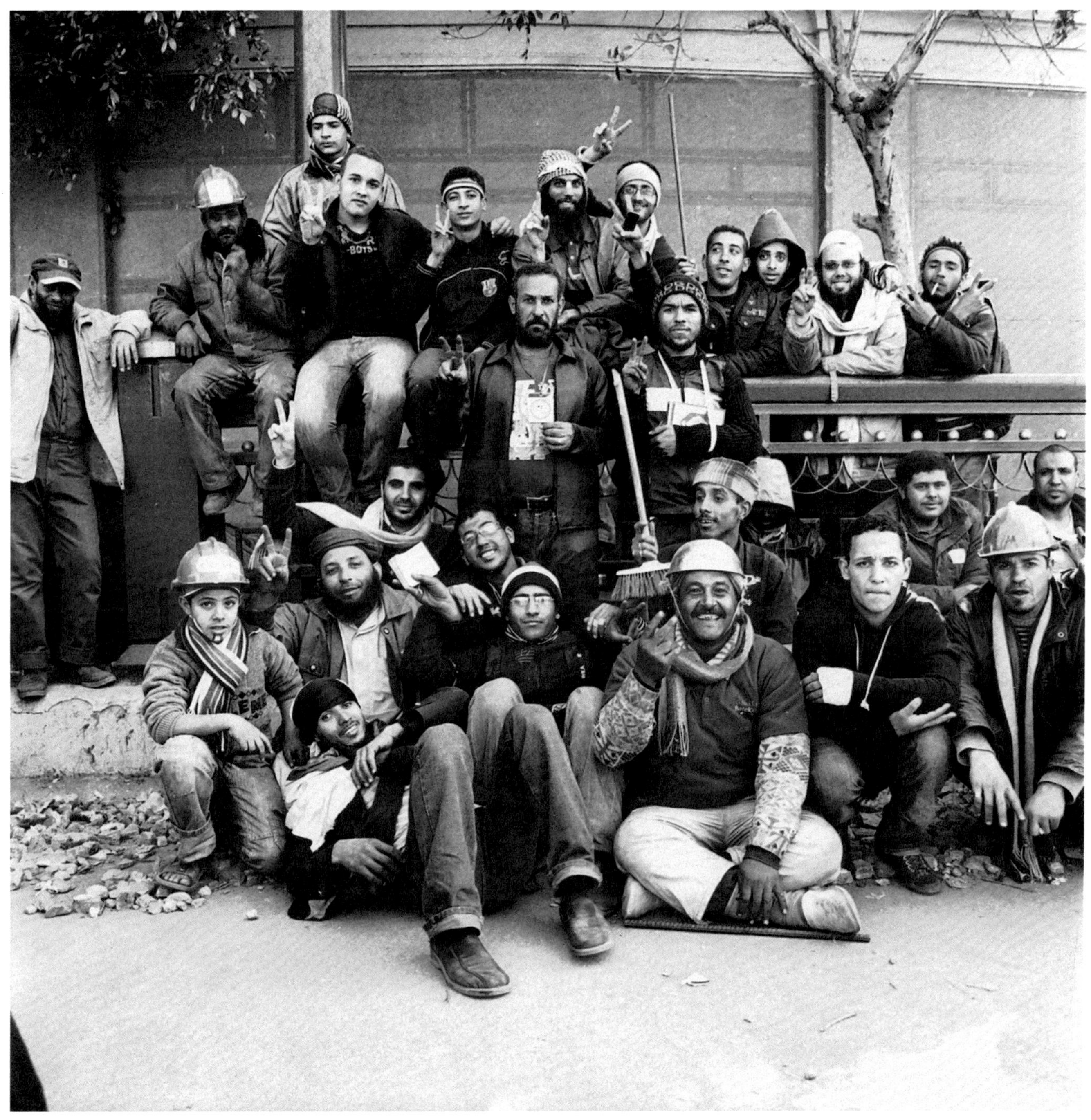

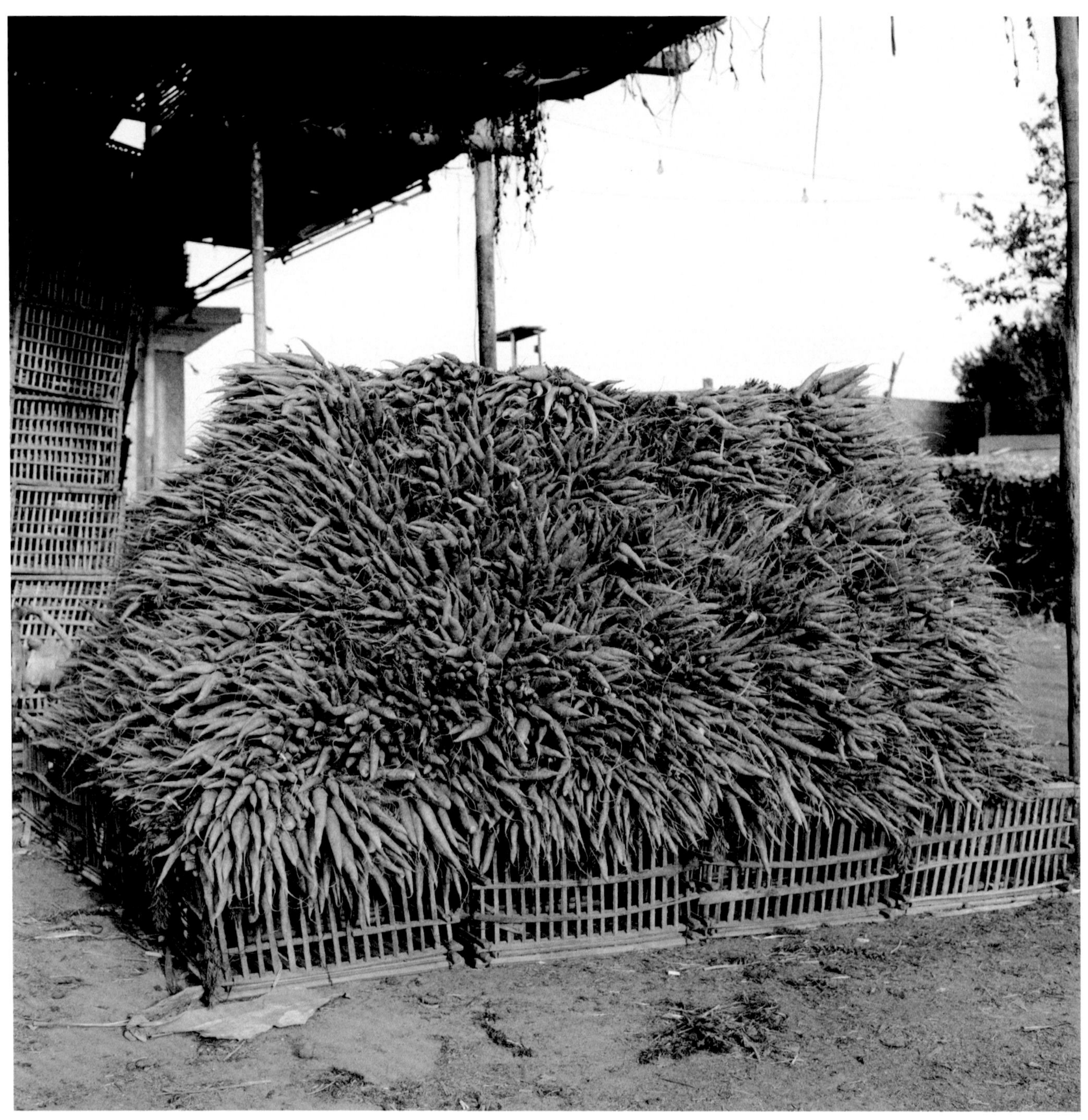

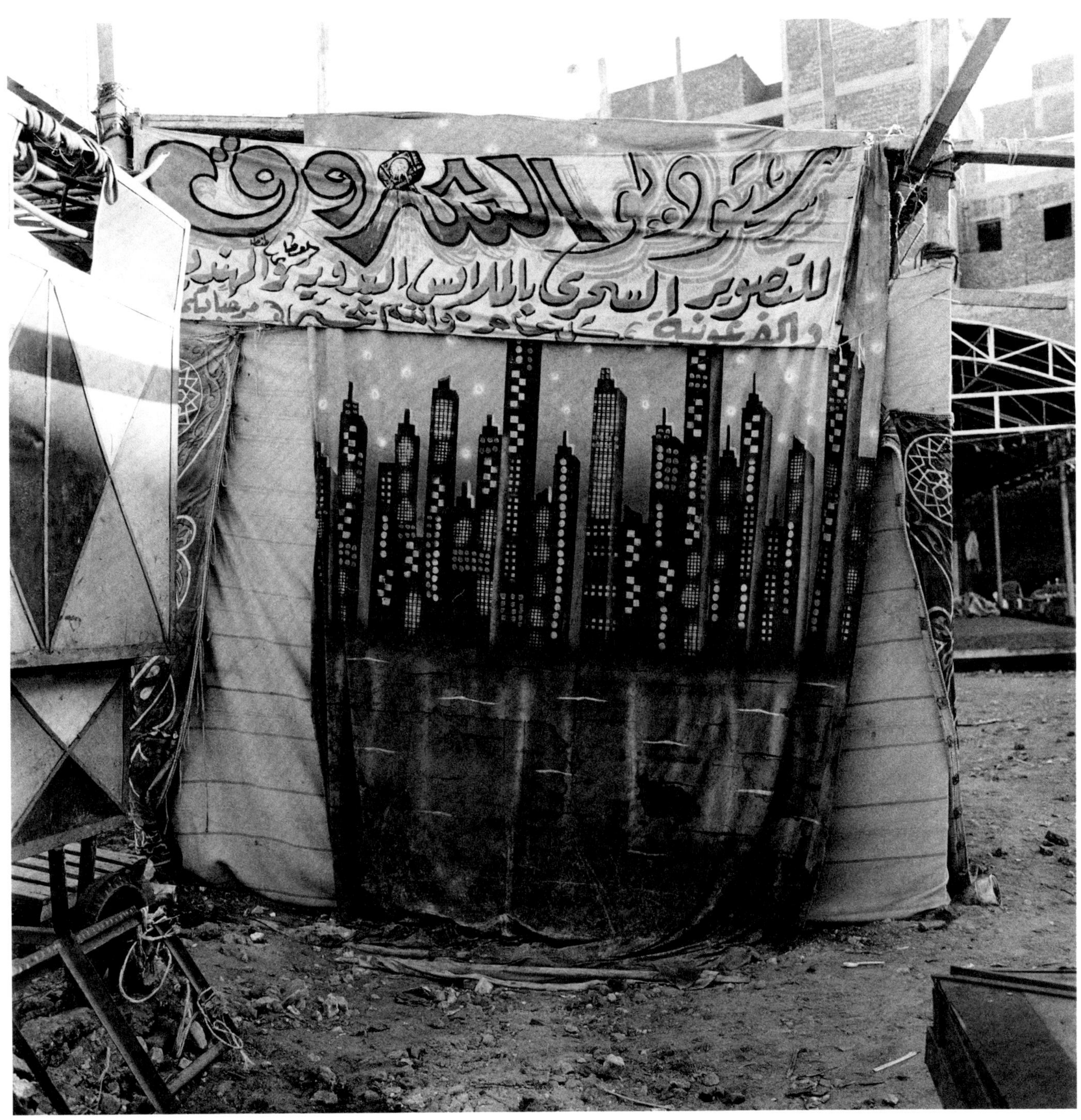

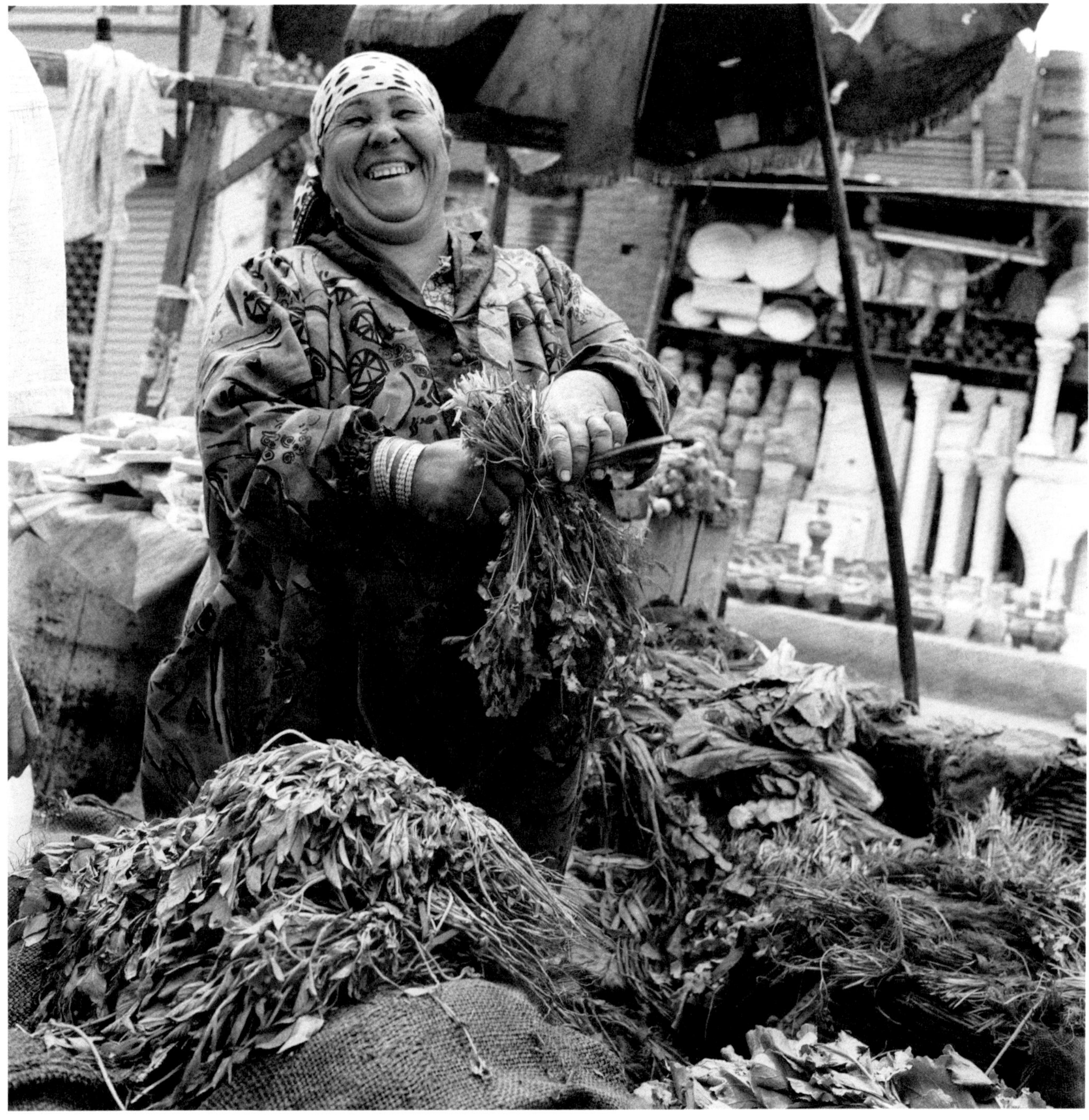

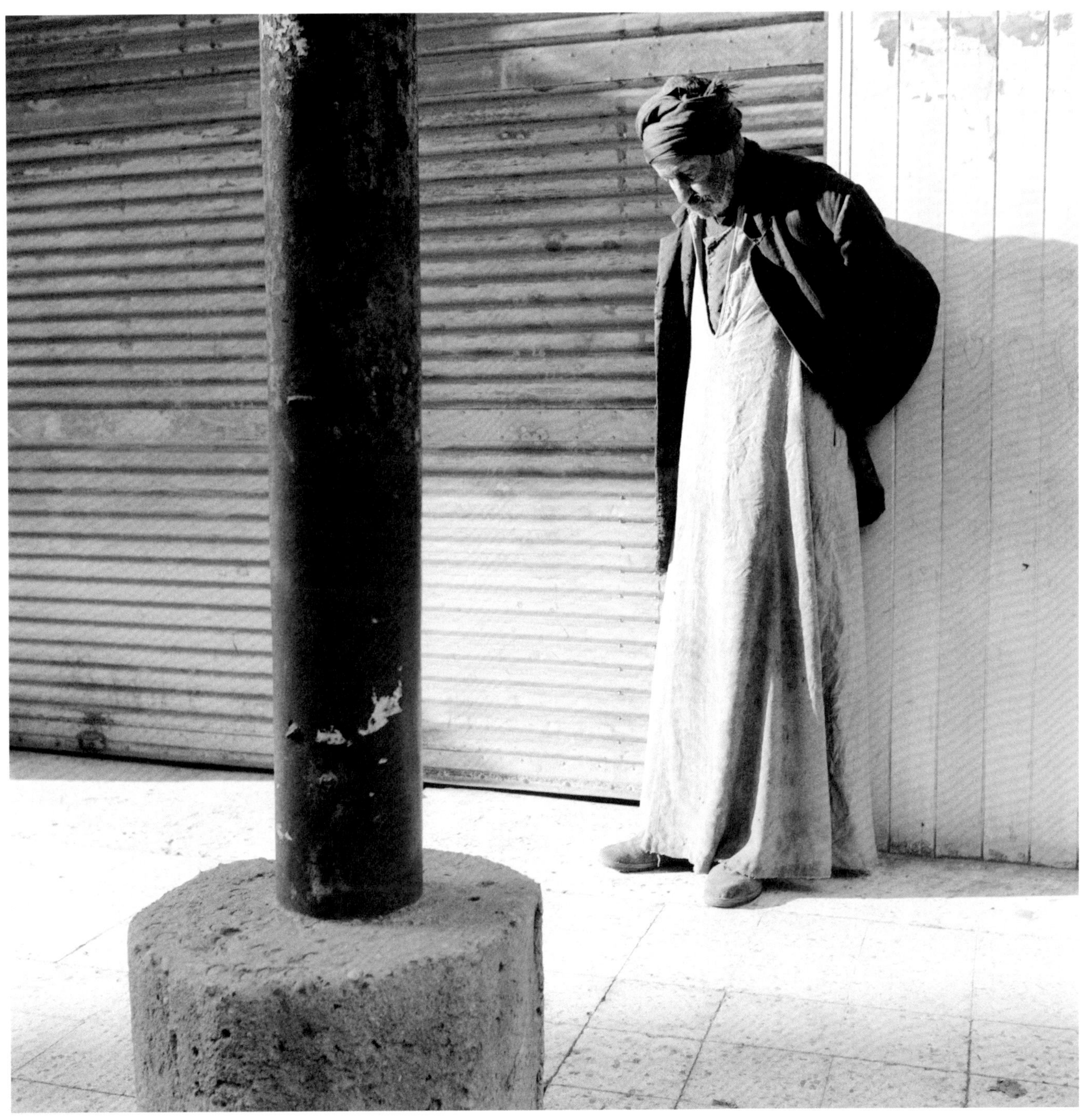

Editorial Note

Alwan and I originally made a first, and larger, selection of images. He then asked me to take responsibility for the final editing and arrangement of the selection. Following Alwan's death, I have both revised and re-composed the book while remaining faithful to the structure and spirit of our original collaboration.

— Shamoon Zamir

Yasser Alwan

May 25, 1964–January 19, 2022

Yasser Alwan was a Cairo-based photographer who first came to Egypt in 1986 under the auspices of the Thomas J. Watson Foundation. He was born in Nigeria to Iraqi parents. His father was a diplomat, and so the family lived in Lebanon and Switzerland before settling in the United States in 1972. A year at the Rhode Island School of Design turned him firmly away from academic art, and after graduating with a BA in French literature from Colby College in 1986, a Watson Foundation fellowship made it possible for Alwan to travel and photograph in Egypt and Sudan for a year, which proved foundational for his decision to pursue photography. Alwan gained an MA in Middle Eastern studies from Georgetown University's Edmund A. Walsh School of Foreign Service in 1992 and returned to the Middle East to live and photograph in Jordan for two years. But it was his first experience of Cairo during the Watson Fellowship year that continued to draw him most. He said of that first experience of the city: "It took my breath away . . . I didn't know it then, but I had fallen in love. And when I came back to the United States, I basically wanted to find a way to return to Cairo." Alwan indeed came back to Cairo in 1994 and lived and worked there until his untimely death on January 19, 2022.

A book and a catalogue of his photos have previously been published: *Scream* (Concord Press, 2000) and *The Liberty of Appearing* (Peacock Imprint, 2008). He also wrote *Imagining Egypt* (Landrock Orient Art Publishers, 2008), a critical commentary on the photographs produced by the studio of Rudolf Franz Lehnert and Ernst Heinrich Landrock. His work has appeared in *Cairo Papers in Social Science* (American University in Cairo Press, 2012), *Alternative Histories* (National Portrait Gallery, 2011), and *The Struggle for Workers Rights in Egypt* (Solidarity Center, 2010). Some of Alwan's work was awarded the Mother Jones International Fund for Documentary Photography (now at the Fifty Crows Foundation) award in 2001. His photos have been exhibited in Cairo, Beirut, Thessaloniki, Paris, London, Frankfurt, New York, San Francisco, and Abu Dhabi.

Shamoon Zamir is professor of literature and art history at New York University Abu Dhabi. His publications include *Helen Levitt: New York, 1939* (MoMA, 2021), *The Gift of the Face: Portraiture and Time in Edward Curtis's The North American Indian* (University of North Carolina Press, 2014), and the co-edited volumes *The Family of Man Revisited: Photography in a Global Age* (I.B. Tauris, 2017), and *The Photobook: From Talbot to Ruscha and Beyond* (I.B. Tauris, 2012).

Egypt Every Day

Shamoon Zamir

Almost all of Yasser Alwan's photographs are portraits. There are many of family and friends. However, the people Alwan most consistently brought into view, in his exhibitions and publications, are individuals he encountered in and around Cairo, in the streets, at the racetrack, in cafes, and in their places of work—tanneries, quarries, bookshops, potteries, the crowded pavements where all kinds of trade are conducted daily. They are, most often, laborers living in conditions of severe poverty, and of near total political and civic dispossession: a fifth estate. The images of friends and family accrued over time, along the way; they were never planned as a project, but they nevertheless add up to a collective portrait of the Egyptian urban middle class, or at least a certain segment of this class. The affectionate sense of familiarity and gentle engagement with the quotidian in these images have taken on the quality of an unexpectedly pressing address at a time when narratives of war, religious violence, the collapse of civil liberties, and the failures of democracy have been crowding out other ways of seeing and understanding the peoples of the Arab world. In contrast to the leisurely making of these photographs, and their slow emergence into purposive design, the portraits of workers and laborers were a conscious project from the very beginning, a determined pursuit: most of them were made during a period of intense work between April 1997 and the end of 1999.

A selection of ninety-nine of these images of laborers and city dwellers was previously brought together in *Scream: Documenting Human Rights*, a photobook self-published by Alwan in January 2000. Alwan's prefatory note to the book clearly states what he strives to achieve in his photographs, and also describes the kind of documentary practice this entails:

> I assume that documenting poverty involves more complexity than a technical description of the living and working conditions of people, otherwise anyone with a still or video camera could describe the surface of poverty with relative ease. This project's central premise is that poverty is only one aspect of a huge number of Egyptians' lives, albeit an important one. One of my goals has been to show conditions that need to be corrected. Another was to photograph aspects of life that need to be appreciated. Only in this way, by showing the possible incongruencies and affinities between the physical, social and emotional realities of such communities, can structural poverty be documented with some accuracy, in its full context. This kind of representation can result in images that do justice to the sense of social cohesion in such communities while not shying away from the difficult conditions in which people live and work. This has meant—*as much as was possible*—photographing poverty from the inside, from within these communities. Such an approach has entailed a way of seeing that goes beyond the directly visible. Only through a way of seeing that requires an 'extended knowing' could I hope to draw out the humanity from those who seem, at first, to have none.[1]

Alwan's images arise out of a sustained relationship with particular locales, and very often also with particular individuals (there are images "based on relationships going back a decade or more," some stretching back over "twenty-five years").[2] Alwan took his time; he lost himself (often quite literally) in the labyrinthine city. It is this sense of a true *inhabiting* (so much more than a "hanging around" in the hope of a good shot) that finds its fulfillment in the human face sedimented with time and experience in the portraits. Even the images that seem to conform more closely to the norms of street photography (images captured as people wait for a bus, for example), seem to be marked by a careful ethics of regard that speaks of the same senses of time, place, and personhood. The project began when Alwan was taken to the horse races "at the once very posh Gezira Club" by a "friend's uncle." Alwan returned "every weekend and eventually started photographing the small community of men who bet at the track." By the end of the third season, Alwan "had met almost every single person who came to bet regularly." It was the time spent with these men that then led Alwan to the neighborhoods of these men (especially Waily and Dar al-Salaam), "the areas where the vast majority of the city's population lives."[3] This is how Alwan describes the way he worked with the communities he photographed:

> I work very, very hard to break down the barriers and their prejudices about why and what I'm trying to do. I show them photographs that I've made in the past. We talk. And I spend an enormous amount of time in the community, learning about what this community is. I'm in a place where I'm entirely off balance, where they are much more comfortable. This is their social setting. And the way that I become comfortable is to slowly over time gain people's trust. One way I do that is to return pictures to people so that they see the kinds of images I make. And that's the real work. If I do that honestly, then I can often make a photograph.[4]

Alwan was himself an outsider–insider. He was born to well-to-do Iraqi parents in Lagos, Nigeria in 1964. After some years in Lebanon and Iraq, the family moved to New York City in 1972. Alwan first came to Egypt in 1986 with the assistance of a grant from the Thomas J. Watson Foundation. The Watson Fellowship enables graduating seniors from a number of US colleges (Alwan had just graduated with a major in French from Colby College) to pursue an original project independently of any affiliation to an academic institution for a year. Alwan came with a plan to photograph and was immediately enthralled by the chaos, "mess," and "frenetic" dance of the city (transcript). But that first experience of living and working in Cairo also made Alwan acutely aware of how "the fact that [his] parents were Iraqi didn't give [him] any kind of access to Egyptian society whatsoever."[5] This is why he studied history and politics at Georgetown University for his master's degree, focusing on Iraq and Egypt: it was preparation for a planned return, the continuation of a personal flight that began to take shape in Alwan's childhood. He recalled that while he was growing up his "name was associated with Yasser Arafat, whom the mainstream media portrayed as the devil incarnate." Alwan resists the recourse to autobiography but could "say without hesitation that mainstream media coverage of the Arab world had a direct impact on [his] life."[6] The plan after the completion of his MA was to go to Iraq, but the aftermath of Iraq's invasion of Kuwait and of the subsequent Gulf War in 1990–91 made that impossible. Some months spent in Jordan failed to produce the connection Alwan had felt for Egypt ("Amman felt like a very, very small town by comparison with Cairo."[7]) So, Alwan found a way to return to Egypt. That was 1994, and from then until his sudden death in 2022 he used photography to be in and of the city and its communities, to be an insider as much as an outsider.

There are other photographers, several of them contemporaries of Alwan's, who have made sympathetic and accomplished portraits of Egyptians. But I don't know of any amongst them who has matched the variety and sustained accumulation of Alwan's portraits, and none who has engaged with working communities and individuals with Alwan's dogged commitment and sustained aesthetic accomplishment. What most sets Alwan's images apart is their achievement of a visual language that can communicate, as much as any photograph possibly can, the ethical experience of meeting another human being across the inequalities of social class and cultural difference. There is an arresting sense of vulnerability in these images: not so much the vulnerability of the people photographed— the fragility imposed on the lives of these people by their economic and social circumstances is never disengaged from self-possession in the portraits—but the vulnerability of the viewer. Alwan, who, like many artists, struggled when asked to speak about his own work, suggested that Judith Butler could serve as a surrogate voice for the concerns that animate it.[8] The same questions that preoccupy Butler's ethics are articulated by Alwan's photographs: "Who counts as human? Whose lives count as lives? And, finally, What *makes for a grievable life*?"[9] For Butler, one cannot confer or receive recognition without an opening up of the enclosure of self-identity, an acceptance of dislocation: "one can give and take recognition only on the condition that one becomes disoriented from oneself by something which is not oneself, that one undergoes a de-centering and 'fails' to achieve self-identity."[10] This de-centering is an essential part of Alwan's experience as photographer: as he said in his description of working among neighborhoods of Cairo's poor, "I'm in a place where I'm entirely off balance." And Alwan's photographs ask the viewer to accept this same loss of balance. I feel unsettled by Alwan's portraits because by showing me so much more than any other photographs of Egypt have shown me, they, paradoxically, make me acutely aware of the opacity of my vision and the limitations of my understanding. Yet it is in these very photographs that I have the sense of beginning to see a face behind the outward appearance of a face: this may be what Alwan means when he says he strives for "a way of seeing that goes beyond the directly visible."[11]

Alwan spoke of his project of photographing Cairo's workers and laborers in terms of incompletion or partialness. According to him, when he started he "was trying to create something like a portrait of the working class. But that's a fairly heavy task to handle. What I did manage to do was to photograph labor."[12] It should come as no surprise that August Sander's ambitious project of creating a collective portrait of the German people in the twentieth century remained a constant point of reference and inspiration for Alwan. But for both Sander and Alwan the scale of their original ambitions offers only part of the explanation for their failure to bring their impossible projects to conclusion. Sander's work was curtailed in the 1930s by Nazi censorship and hostility. Meanwhile Alwan's relations with the Egyptian state's security apparatus were marked by

a similar precarity. In 1986, during his first visit to Egypt, when a state of emergency had been imposed following the assassination of President Sadat, he "spent three days in a state security prison for making pictures."[13] Then in the 1990s, when he started focusing on labor, the state security service had Alwan followed for three months, simply because the kind of photography he was pursuing was unusual enough to arouse undefined suspicions. Alwan's dark room was broken into and some of his pictures confiscated. More damagingly, state security "systematically tried to destroy" Alwan's "relationships with people"; the people he was photographing were "threatened and terrified," so much so that they "didn't want to see [him] again."[14] In other words, as Alwan affirmed:

> Photographing in this particular social setting is threatening to the power structure of Egypt. And that makes the environment very, very difficult to work in because on the one hand people imagine you are doing something wrong and on the other hand, the state tries to prevent this work from coming into existence. (transcript)

Except for the brief moment of liberalization made possible by Egypt's Arab Spring in 2011, increasing state paranoia and the continuing assaults on the remaining vestiges of a liberal civil society in Egypt made it impossible for Alwan to pursue his kind of photography with any regularity since the early 2000s.

But even if his portraits of the working people of Cairo were for Alwan only a fragment of an as-yet-uncompleted project, they already constitute a body of work that can reshape our understanding of contemporary Egypt and its visual histories. Moreover they are photographs that securely deserve to be part of present-day discussions about photography's engagement with human rights.

*

Like most of Alwan's portraits of Egyptian workers and laborers, the photograph of the man with the raised hammer (p. 17), seated on a ragged mat on a dusty floor, is one that has been negotiated and posed; it is not, however, *staged,* even though the arrest of action and the turn towards the camera impart to the image something of the quality of a tableau vivant. There is in this portrait, as in many others by Alwan, an unresolved movement between time and its suspension, between the historicity of labor and the refusal to treat the face as merely the object of history. The face and the hammer work as two centers of gravity within the visual field of the image. The hammer's weighty materiality, and the visual insistence created by its bright circular surface (its own "face" so to speak), do not exert a pull equal to the disarming openness of the man's face, but they are nevertheless strong enough to animate the photograph with a dialectical sense. Alwan's portrait does not reduce the man to the work he does (he is not a type, "the Egyptian laborer"), nor does it allow him to pull away entirely from the conditions of his work. This leaves the relationship of self and labor, between agency and determinism, an open question, so that the image also encourages the viewer to interrogate the adequacy of empathy in fully understanding what is seen.

The human figure and face are at the center of Alwan's pictures; they are almost always framed by the conditions of labor, but never presented as only illustrations of the effects of the environments in which they work. In his work, Alwan rarely includes wide views of work environments to help establish explanatory contexts for his portraits, which means that the exact nature of the work being done in the photographs (as with the man with the hammer) is often not entirely clear: I will return to the question of why Alwan does this below.[15] Within the limits set by this practice of visual framing, the individuals photographed are at liberty to pose themselves. Each portrait is, therefore, an act of self-presentation to some significant degree. The men (and given the prohibitions on photographing women among the working class in Egyptian culture, it is nearly always men) mostly turn to face the camera, which means the work they are doing is momentarily suspended. In some of the portraits this is simply a consequence of the pause needed for the taking of the photograph. But in others there is much more a sense that the forms of labor we are seeing are being performed as essential aspects of the presentation of self; what we seem to be seeing in these images is not work being done but work being acted out. This is palpably the case in the portrait of the man with disfigured skin holding a crowbar. This man worked in the same place as the man with the hammer. Given his skin condition, Alwan was unsure that the man would want to be photographed, so he initially avoided doing so. But then Alwan was approached by the man himself, who felt left out when all his workmates were being invited to participate in Alwan's novel project. The pose at work is therefore self-chosen. The jacket and hat, even if they are the clothes this man normally wears at work, contrast with the mismatched and worn-out shoes, and bring to the rigid acting out an oddly spruced up sense of self. The crowbar and the hammer, both held in mid-air, contribute in very similar ways to the visual dynamics of their respective pictures, and the poised hammer seems no less a part of a performance that uses labor as a vehicle for a self-presentation than is the case with the crowbar in the portrait of the man with disfigured skin. This deployment, we could say appropriation, of the very labor that defines the poverty to which these men are consigned may seem strange. But it should not be read as an assertion of "the dignity of labor," by either the men photographed, or by the photographer. It is more properly a recognition of labor as a marshaling of resources necessary to secure continued living without accepting abject defeat; it is a form of persistence, visible to the photographer as a kind of desperate heroism but unlikely to be consciously articulated as such by the men in the photographs themselves, even if felt and understood as such by them on some level. Perdurance is imaged as something achieved and secured through labor, wrested from the indifference of the present, rather than merely a living through it. Alongside this sense of historicity, the photographs equally, and paradoxically, invite us into a suspension of time, the effect of a photographic encounter that is shaped by Alwan's slow pace of attention and careful unfolding within the space of a reciprocal generosity between photographer and subject.

The lack of reserve in the man-with-the-hammer's face offers little resistance to the viewer. But this is exceptional among Alwan's portraits. More usually, something is held back or put up, even as the photographer's invitation is accepted, so that the viewer is compelled to make an altogether greater effort to find a way into the photograph. One has only to compare the portrait of the man with the hammer with that of the man with a pickaxe at the limestone quarry (p. 13) to see this. The quarry worker has lifted himself out of an immersion in work, an abandonment of the self to the oblivion of fatiguing routine, to face the camera. The squint of the eyes and the grimace of the face are not only a reflex against the harsh sunlight, but also the sign of a perplexity, a curiosity. Who is this guy with a camera? Why does he hang around here all the time? Why is he taking pictures? And these questions translate into a question posed to the viewer: What are you looking at, and why? We know that the very next moment the man will turn around and go back to his work. But there is just the possibility within the symbolic range available in the photograph of imagining that he will turn more fully towards us, pickaxe still lifted. There is, in other words, just the hint in the image of a potential and unaccountable aggression. To speak of this possibility even as a hint, though, may already be to overstate the fleeting effects of Alwan's image work. It may be more faithful to Alwan's art to say that the gesture of the lifted pickaxe underlines the reserve, which can also be a form of repulse, caught in the man's face. And even in this description there is the potential for rigidity, as if reserve, repulse, and hesitation were not in a continuum with open giving, a continuum that is caught by Alwan at different stages in different portraits.

It is possible to force this picture into a revolutionary reading: introducing Alwan's photographs for an exhibition in London, John Molyneux wrote of the quarry worker that "he is about to smite the limestone not the international bourgeoisie . . . and yet"[16] Molyneux is sensitive to the politics of Alwan's portraits, but in these photographs the rage against injustice is always channelled through a practice of visual composure that refuses the viewer the comforting legibility of the exaggerated gesture or effect (and for this very reason Alwan's choice of *Scream* as the title for his first photobook seems all too vocal). When Alwan photographed the protesters at Tahrir Square during Egypt's Arab Spring (pp. 94–97), his portraits maintained their characteristic stillness; they resolutely refused the dramaturgy of political protest precisely because Alwan's portraits have in a sense been picturing the revolution all along. These are the faces of a long revolution, one that unfolds at a pace and in forms that the popular media are unable either to recognize or represent. Alwan photographs the ordinary, the day to day,

but his images are not mundane. They engage the viewer with what had been visible to Alwan's eyes for many years: a human reality of fortitude, anger, persistence, good humor, and pride that is the reality of Egypt's everyday.

The man with the raised hammer works in a tannery, as does his colleague with the crowbar (p. 16). The tanneries use wooden frames to hang hides. These frames are regularly disassembled and reassembled. The job of the man with the crowbar is to prize out the nails; what the man with the hammer is doing is to straighten each nail, one by one, so that it can be used again. If you look carefully at the wooden planks behind the man with the crowbar, you can see all the perforations that record a history of this use and re-use.

This ecology of recycling is entirely typical of the substrata of the Egyptian economy. It is evident everywhere—in electronic repair shops, at building and plumbing merchants, and in the city's sprawling flea markets—but it is represented most famously by the *zabbaleen*, or garbage collectors. These men and women, concentrated in particular around the Muqattam Hills in a community of some 60,000 or more, are, in Maria Golia's words, "one of Cairo's most exemplary communities":

> The *zabbaleen* . . . have for generations made it their business to collect garbage and live off what they recycle. The work involves the entire family; men do the hauling while women sort the garbage at home, mostly by hand. The *zabbaleen* find value in everything, identifying sixteen categories of trash, including types of metal, paper, glass, cloth, organic waste (fed to animals), bones (used for glue) and *naqda*, odd articles like 'toys, vases, artificial flowers, cutlery and miscellaneous objects run by small motors.' Finally, *rabish* is the residual stuff that goes to the municipal dump, the real garbage. Egypt boasts one of the highest waste recovery rates in the world, 80 per cent, because of the courage, skill and resourcefulness of the *zabbaleen*.[17]

The *zabbaleen* represent an economy that is very particular to Cairo, but this is an economy that cannot be disarticulated from the global ascendancy of neoliberal financial austerity campaigns spearheaded by the International

Monetary Fund (IMF), the World Trade Organization (WTO), and the World Bank, to which so called "developing" countries and "emerging" economies have been subjected. As Karen Pfeifer argues, the "structural adjustment programs" (or SAPs) enforced by the IMF, WTO, and the World Bank, whatever their success in reducing inflation and budget deficits, or in servicing national debts, have without fail exacerbated unemployment and inequality, and damaged the concern for human welfare that should be at the heart of development policy.[18] When Alwan first came to Egypt in the 1980s, the country was gripped by a severe economic crisis. And when he returned in the 1990s, the new economic measures designed to overcome this crisis, inspired by the major international financial organizations, were being put in process, with disastrous results. Between 1981 and 1991, "the percentage of the poor" in rural Egypt "rose from 16.1 to 28.6 percent . . . while in urban areas it rose from 18.2 to 20.3 percent." If "a higher poverty line, including those deemed moderately poor," were applied, "the percentage rose from 26.9 in 1981–82 to 39.2 percent in rural areas, and from 33.5 to 39 percent in urban ones."[19] The economic reforms of the 1990s appear to have accelerated these trends. According to "an independent analysis of consumption surveys from 1990–91 and 1995–96 (the SAP period) . . . the overall poverty rate, defined as the ability to purchase a minimally nutritious diet, rose from 21 per cent to 44 per cent of the population." The staff of the IMF itself estimated that in 1995 the rate of unemployment in Egypt could have been as high as 22 percent of the population.[20] The electoral corruption, the assaults on the press, and the repression, often violent, of political opposition that Egyptians have witnessed since the 1980s have, to a large extent, been corollaries of the country's ongoing economic catastrophe.

The t-shirt worn by the man with the hammer catches the entrapment of the lives of ordinary Egyptian working people within the global economic machine. The writing on the t-shirt is the trademarked slogan of the Lee Jeans company: "Made to Fit Better – Since 1889," however, because of the way the folds in the cloth appear in the image, the eye scans the words more immediately as "made it better." Either way, the text opens up the image to a range of painful ironies. Who or what has been made to fit better and into

what? *Who* has made *what* better? One thing is certain: the slogan does not herald any improvement in the human lot of the man pictured at his extraordinary labor of recycling old nails. And the final irony may not be that Egyptian cotton, which helped fuel the industrial revolution in Europe, and which has continued to supply the international clothing trade, here returns home via a global corporate brand; it may instead be that the t-shirt is most likely an Egyptian knock-off, an imitation of a branded global commodity.

For Charles Baudelaire, writing in the middle of the nineteenth century, the ragpicker became an emblem of modern life, a figure that stood against the commodity and consumerism:

> Here we have a man whose job it is to gather the day's refuse in the capital. Everything that the big city has thrown away, everything it has lost, everything it has scorned, everything it has crushed underfoot he catalogues and collects. He collates the annals of intemperance, the capharnaum of waste. He sorts things out and selects judiciously: he collects like a miser guarding a treasure, refuse which will assume the shape of useful or gratifying objects between the jaws of the goddess of Industry.[21]

The fact that Alwan's tannery workers or the *zabbaleen* can continue to serve the same emblematic function within the histories of Egyptian modernization and economic development as Baudelaire's ragpicker did for European capitalism almost a hundred and fifty years ago is a telling, and dispiriting, comment on the state of the nation.

If Cairo's recyclers and garbage collectors form a social periphery from which we can better see the true nature of the economic system they help to service and sustain, they also help to demarcate the limitations of the visual field within which Egypt has come to be seen and known beyond the long-standing fascination with its archaeological past. As Alwan himself explained, "because of international development projects," the area where the *zabbaleen* live "has been one of the most visited neighbourhoods by foreigners and local NGOs. And the photographs that have resulted are some of the most superficial photographs of poverty that have been made in Egypt." But because of "the world-wide NGO system, these photographs are seen all over. There are books on the *zabbaleen* and films on the *zabbaleen* and so on."[22] The tanners and limestone workers of greater Cairo have received their fair share of the same kind of attention and have also been the subjects of the same kinds of image making. And these images are not always the work only of foreign photojournalists; they are just as often made by Egyptian photographers, either working for news agencies and magazines, or as independent documentarists.[23]

For Alwan, what matters above all are the visual and ethical consequences of different kinds of photographic practice and vision; he is not, first and foremost, concerned with judging the intentions of photographers or degrees of sincerity. The differences between photojournalism and social documentary on the one hand, and orientalist and travel photography on the other, between, say, the realism of the former and the romanticism of the latter, are less important than the fact that all of these photographic modes tend to produce images that have the air of being pre-scripted—in the case of photojournalism, of course, this is very often literally the case since editors tell the photographers what to photograph. Photographers of the newsworthy event, of a current social "problem," of striking monuments, of the timeless *fellahin*, tend to photograph what they already know, or imagine they know. Alwan instead uses his camera as a means of discovering unexpected experiences and realities.

*

It is ironic then that members of the Egyptian middle and upper classes see in Alwan's images something of the same sensationalism, the exposé effect, that he himself withdrew from in photojournalism, though in the case of these Egyptians the response has less to do with the ethics of image-making or with how a photograph communicates, than with a national pride that, one suspects, obscures class self-consciousness and guilt. When Alwan first exhibited his photographs in Cairo in January 2000, on the occasion of the publication of *Scream*, "the reaction was quite vocal and quite harsh." Alwan was told that he "was a foreigner making Egyptians look bad and photographing the wrong kind of people."[24] And he met with the same

reaction from Egyptians when he showed his photographs in London or Paris. Alwan believed that until the "January 25th Revolution" of 2011, "there was . . . an absolute state of denial in the country about the social situation of most people." Speaking in 2012, he was hopeful that things would begin to change; an optimism that did not survive the subsequent rolling back of the populist uprising.

The portraits of friends and family have neither been exhibited in Egypt nor widely shown outside Egypt, and few have been previously published other than on Alwan's own website. It is difficult to say what the bourgeois Egyptians offended by Alwan's portraits of workers are likely to make of his representations of members of their own class. Alwan's middle class is, of course, a very particular segment of the middle class: largely liberal in its social, political, and religious attitudes, and above comfortable in front of Alwan's camera without retreating behind the protective masks of prescribed identity. There is nothing to offend or shock here, but these portraits will not pass muster as images of the kind of bourgeois decorum welcomed by the state as representative of national identity. The portraits of friends and family show us a world very far removed from the world of manual laborers and street vendors. There is, unsurprisingly, a far greater sense of relaxed intimacy in these images, and the immensely humane humor that one glimpses in some of the portraits of workers is much more fully at play. And yet, there is also a more acute and pervasive sense of melancholy in these portraits than in those of the dispossessed, a melancholy that is perhaps a class luxury and the sign of a dispossession of a different order.

What the portraits of friends and family members share with those of the workers is a compositional reserve and formality that are characteristic of Alwan's work, and that have been slowly achieved until they have become an intuitive and habitual stance rather than a studied effect. But, on one level at least, this compositional attitude serves a very different purpose in the portraits of friends and family than that served by the portraits of workers. In the latter, Alwan seeks out a level of familiarity with his subjects that will take his work beyond the glancing views of poverty and the poor that he saw as the prevalent modes of photojournalism and social documentary. The sense of reserve that pervades Alwan's visual composition is here a safeguard against both false intimacy and the reduction of his subjects to types. In the portraits of friends and family members, by contrast, this same formal reserve seems to serve to hold back the pressure of easy intimacy with the subjects Alwan is photographing, a pressure under which the images could easily collapse into the casual familiarity and personal meanings of the family album.

In the preceding discussion, I have used August Sander as a point of reference for Alwan's work. Sander and Walker Evans were two photographers to whom Alwan turned frequently in our many conversations over the years. Alwan had a wide-ranging knowledge of photography and he sought out work by photographers old and new. His tastes were catholic, his judgements careful and precise. He found little to hold his attention for long in the art and documentary photography from the modern or the contemporary Arab world.[25] But in the studio, amateur, and family photographs from the region (p. 55), especially those from the first half of the twentieth century, he found ways of making photographs and modes of self-presentation that deeply shaped his own efforts to find new ways to picture encounter and selfhood in present-day Egypt.

Alwan regularly scoured Cairo's flea markets and secondhand bookstores for prints and negatives from old photographers' studios, family albums, and even glass-plate negatives. The intuition that there was something to be learned from these quotidian images, which were now a visual detritus, came from Alwan's own family photographs: "A photograph of my mother and aunt from Beirut in 1954 has been part of my life as long as I can remember, he wrote in 2017, "so I knew that there had to be personal photographs in Egypt."[26] I saw this photograph on Alwan's desk in his apartment in Cairo, and as I recall it pictured two young women in a head-and-shoulder shot, set against a light, plain background, both women with neatly-set hair, in identical dresses, their faces angled to left. They seemed similar enough to have been twins, and this visual unsettling of the boundaries of identity deepened the sense in the dual portrait of a serene unspoken communication across a bond of kinship. Remarkably, we see a version of this very effect in a number of Alwan's own dual portraits, especially of children, where physical symmetry and resemblance are often used as a motif (pp. 66–67).

Over roughly twenty years, Alwan collected around 3,000 images:

Finding these photographs was serendipity, but collecting them became a passion. I never planned to collect photographs like these, preferring to make my own. But these images drew me into a kindred relationship. They were made by men and women who were my kin—the photographers who worked in Egypt professionally and as amateurs long before my arrival. They showed me how people liked to present themselves to the camera, especially when poses, props, and costumes recurred over time. These presentations usually remained in the realm of the private. These were the photographs that families would share with their friends when they came to visit, or the wedding photograph that would be on display at home. They were not meant for mass consumption. Yet they reflected prevailing tastes, fashions, and attitudes.

Because I saw them as part of Egypt's history and society, these historical documents contained lessons for me as I was making my own portraits here. Through them I could glimpse my adopted country in a way that wasn't otherwise available to me. I was looking at my larger Egyptian family and examining the ways professionals and amateurs used the medium when people weren't afraid to be photographed 'as they were.'[27]

In almost all these photographs there is a mutually supportive balance between the composure of the subjects and the undemonstrative composition of the photographers, which is characteristic of early studio photography. It is a balance and a dialogue that Alwan developed in striking ways into his own visual grammar. The studio portraits mostly display a limited repertoire of poses and gestures, but somehow without becoming repetitive: the subject in their Sunday best, seated or standing against a painted background that shows an elegant interior or a foreign landscape; the newly-married couple in their wedding clothes; the patriarch of the family with his wife beside him, his children standing behind or seated at his feet; the solitary child in clothes that clearly mark a special occasion. But every so often jokey humor and surreal comedy break through: a man in an elegant suit turns out his trouser pockets in a Chaplinesque gesture signaling that he is broke, and three men, also elegantly suited, imitate a musical trio with what appear to be toy instruments, party hats on their heads, one seated on a rocking horse, another holding a tambourine in one hand and a large doll in the other. The bizarre nature of this last example only further highlights the mute mysteries one finds in almost all the found images.[28]

That there is in these photographs, mysteriously, no contradiction between the "as they were" and the theatricality of self-presentation—that, I think, is what most drew Alwan to these portraits. The paradoxical play of revelation and performance evident in these early photographs is no longer available to us, as part of a globally pervasive visual regime whereby anxieties about privacy cordon off the public uses of photographs, but especially in Egypt where the strict state control of photography and of social norms now severely restricts all forms of visual freedom.[29] This is why these found images were, for Alwan, "the material remains of a social sensibility that is no longer apparent, or that no longer exists." Though Alwan adds himself that they "perhaps never existed at all except in the imagination of photographers and their sitters," it is the possibility of that collaborative imagining that his own photographs strive to realize. Alwan was equally and acutely aware that the workers who became the subjects of his photography were not part of this found visual archive which was, given the costs of photography, inevitably an archive of the Egyptian middle class.

*

Though Alwan recognized and actively fashioned his kinship with the amateur and jobbing photographers of a bygone era, he did not give into a fiction of identification: he was unequivocal in articulating his own work as art, albeit an art that stood for him well apart from the art "scene" and the art world he saw as ascendent around him, both nationally and globally. Alwan spoke of his work as a form of documentary. This was the convenience of shorthand, and it is evident in conversation that he was very much drawn to Walker Evans's distinction between "documentary" and "documentary style" as a way of describing his own photographic practice more precisely. In a 1971 interview, late on in his long career, Evans argued that documentary was "a very sophisticated and misleading word. And not very clear." He insisted that one needed "a sophisticated ear to receive that word. The term should be *documentary style*." For Evans, "a document has use, whereas art is really useless." In his own case, Evans thought that being called a "documentary photographer" only made sense if "a sophisticated knowledge of the distinction" between documentary and documentary style was kept in play. He further accepted the label of documentary as a disguise: "Very often I'm doing one thing when I'm thought to be doing another." But as Evans's biographer James R. Mellows notes, "that subversive admission had further ambiguities. One of the transcripts of the tapes reads: 'And very often I'm doing one thing and I thought I was doing another'—a more mundane alternative."[30] Alwan was never as arch as Evans but the unresolved tension between document and art, between usefulness and a resistance to instrumentalist utility, between (as the preface to *Scream* puts it) the reformist desire to show "conditions that need to be corrected" and the more elusive ambition of developing "a way of seeing that goes beyond the directly visible"—even between seemingly doing one thing while perhaps doing another, so between conscious plan and a practitioner's instinct: these are all equally animating energies in Alwan's work.

Alwan's ambivalence and hesitation about documentary is signalled by the way he presented his work: in print, in exhibition, and online. Alwan avoided narrative explanation and provided only minimal textual framing for his images; a practice respected in the present publication. In *Scream* there is only a page-long preface, and this is placed *behind* the fold of the front cover, so that what one sees first is a photograph, the text emerging only when the cover with the image is folded back. When Alwan did write or talk about his work, he spoke about how he came to his project, and the general conditions in which he had worked; he offered no sociological or historical accounts to contextualize the portraits. The closest he came to this is the almost random list of statistics presented as a one-page "Index" at the very beginning of *Scream*: the daily wage of a railroad gang worker (9 LE) juxtaposed against the price of a 35mm, 36 exposure

Kodak TMAX 400 ASA film (11.70 LE); the unchanging low levels of literacy between 1986 and 1996; the "average cost of one square meter of residential real estate in Zamalek" (a middle-class neighborhood) (2,500 LE) compared to the "cost of a 65m² apartment on Fath St. in the Gezira neighbourhood or Dar al-Salaam" (39,000 LE); "the amount of dollars that the average tourist spent during a seven-day stay in Egypt in 1997" ($910), and the "percentage of this amount compared to an average Egyptian's yearly income in 1997" (73); and so on. As the preface to *Scream* makes clear, the statistics are not provided as an explanation ("numbers can . . . deceive") but rather as an aid, as a series of mini shocks, for those unfamiliar with the social realities of contemporary Egypt.

In the photographs themselves there is little that approximates the strategies of the traditional photo-essay. The focus on workers may provide a loose organizing topic or theme, however Alwan rarely produced the kinds of images usually required by photo-essays to establish contexts and explanatory frameworks: there are almost no establishing shots of the spaces of work, no consistent alteration of group and individual portraits, no sequencing of images to illustrate a particular work process through all its stages from beginning to end, no obvious indication of the causes of economic deprivation through the picturing of corporate or state agents. What we are instead presented with, both in exhibitions and online, is one portrait followed by another, and then another, and another. The effect is not monotonous: in Alwan's portraits our encounter with the intensity of each face opens for us the sense of a world made newly and repeatedly unfamiliar in its human dimensions. The experience is emotionally exhausting, especially when the images are seen in exhibition. Alwan preferred to print most of his portraits 1m x 1m (with the rest 50cm x 50 cm). The large format helps produce a state of absorption and immersion that sharpens and deepens the viewer's affective experience, and at the same time projects this intensity as a disturbance or tremor into the contemplative space of the gallery.

The precise film and camera Alwan used are essential to the effects that he achieves in his portraits. When Alwan began to photograph, he was using standard 35mm film. But in the mid-1990s, soon after he began to photograph at the Gezira Club, he switched to 120 film and a camera with a waist-level viewfinder—first a Rolleiflex, and then a Hasselblad. The waist level viewfinder means that Alwan looked down to focus rather than having his face behind the camera, so that he could maintain direct eye contact with the person he was photographing. And the 120 film (which is 60mm wide) afforded Alwan the luxury of a medium format, square negative that produces images with far greater tonality and detail than a 35mm negative, and also less distortion, so that what we see in the final print is much closer to what the eye actually sees. And even though the larger negative creates a wider angle, the image still appears more natural, reducing the depth of field and isolating the face or the figure in space, bringing it into a more intimate presence in the visual field of the photograph. In the rectangular, landscape format of 35mm film, there is often the sense of a face or a figure being *in* the environment pictured around it, being determined by it; in the square format as Alwan uses it the face and figure appear to gather the environment around themselves more, to somehow configure it, so that what is visible of the world in the picture appears as an attribute of the person seen even as it clearly also a defining context for personhood.

As noted earlier, Alwan is not the only photographer to have produced sympathetic portraits of Egyptians that depart from the conventions of received imagery: from the late 1980s to the early 2000s, more or less the same years in which Yasser Alwan most actively pursued his project on Cairo's citizens and workers, Dorothy Bohm, Katia Boyadjian, Denis Dailleux, Carlos Freire, Jean Pierre Ribière, and Frédéric Soreau all produced photobooks about Egypt (some in collaboration with writers). Each of these photobooks is characterized by a personal visual engagement with the country and its people that is neither reportage nor reformist project, and each contains a number of notable portraits of individuals.[31] But these portraits usually punctuate larger visual narratives or ensembles: there are city and rural views, or both; architecture, old and new, alternates with people; medium or long distance illustrations of agriculture or industrial activity book-end and outnumber portraits of people; and these portraits are often head-and-shoulder close-ups taken against a wall or some other plain backdrop, so without the sense of a particular location. Occasionally we do see individuals at their labor or in a work environment, but in these images the concern with work as such is incidental. The portraits serve to provide the human dimension for what are in effect portraits of the nation or its cities. In the work of each one of these photographers, culture, space, and history are used far more broadly and visibly as coordinates for locating individuals, and for orienting the viewer-reader, than in the work of Alwan. In making such comparisons, my intention is not to pass any adverse judgement on these other photographers; the comparisons are simply useful for drawing attention to what it is that sets Alwan's work apart from almost all other photographic engagements with Egypt that of which I know, even those that have themselves sought to dismantle long-established visual clichés.

In this regard the most useful point of comparison is perhaps Paul Strand and James Aldridge's *Living Egypt,* from 1969.[32] This work, very much a product of an era that was witness to several former colonies emerging into independence, stops short of prediction but is nevertheless full of optimism about Nasser's project of modernizing Egypt, the very project we see in ruins in Alwan's images. Not surprisingly, the construction of the Aswam Dam, nearing completion in 1969, features as the centerpiece of the narrative of industrial development and progress. There are a good number of very striking and fine portraits by Strand, both men and women, all head-and-shoulder shots of the kind described above. While the delicacy and care of Strand's engagement with the Egyptians he photographs is never in any doubt, there is also no question that these portraits are made to serve the larger narrative of the book, driven especially by Aldridge's text but also by Strand's construction of a visual equivalent. The portraits that appear in the book's latter part are in modern dress. But the preceding kind, in the majority, show individuals in traditional clothes. The projected narrative is obvious: interspersed between photographs that chart a movement from rural life and agriculture to industrialization, from country to city, the portraits in sequence propose a transformation of the *fellahin,* the repositories of Egyptian-ness, into the citizens of a modern republic in the process of being built.

Why is it then that in his work Alwan resists explanatory narrative and the textual elaboration of context, preferring instead the cumulative intensity of the photographic portrait experienced as a series of fragments? How Alwan photographed the people he photographed, and how he presented his photographs was an effort to give visual form to an ethics that is critical of totalizing accounts of personhood. For Alwan, such accounts, because they pursue coherence in their representations of the individual, are not capacious or generous enough to let people emerge in all their individual variety and with all their contradictions. This is why Alwan was suspicious of much of the existing photography of Egypt, from orientalist genre views, to photojournalism, travelogues, or social documentary. Butler is again useful here. She is wary, like Alwan I think, of "the way in which narrative coherence may foreclose an ethical resource—namely, an acceptance of the limits of knowability in oneself and others." Butler further argues that in accepting the coherence of biography or autobiography:

we may be preferring the seamlessness of the story to something we might tentatively call the truth of the person, a truth that, to a certain degree . . . might well become more clear in moments of interruption, stoppage, open-endedness—in enigmatic articulations that cannot easily be translated into narrative form.[33]

I don't think it distorts the meanings of either Butler's ethics or of Alwan's photographs if we transfer Butler's argument about the relationship of narrative and personhood to Alwan's portraits. Alwan uses the sense of "interruption" and "stoppage" that is inherent to the fragmentary form of the photograph to good effect, even though dramatic gesture or action are not his subjects; this is why his images so often seem pervaded by a sense of suspended time. In these fragmented and suspended moments Alwan seems to be seeking out precisely "something we might tentatively call the truth of the person" he is photographing. It seems entirely fitting to describe Alwan's portraits as "enigmatic articulations that cannot easily be translated into narrative form," as long as we bear in mind that this is not just the description of an aesthetic practice, but also of an ethics.

1   The publication of *Scream* was financially supported by the embassies of the Netherlands and Switzerland in Cairo, and the book was printed, unfortunately poorly, by the Concord Press. The prefatory note is printed on the inside of the front and back covers, in English and Arabic respectively. The only other substantial presentation of Alwan's photographs in print has been the catalogue for his exhibition at the Foyles Bookstore gallery in London in 2008: *The Liberty of Appearing: Photographs of Egyptian Working People* (Portsmouth: Peacock Imprint, 2008), edited by Richard Peacock, with an introduction by John Molyneux. A smaller catalogue of a 2014 exhibition in Doha, which included both portraits of working people and also of friends and their families, is available online: issuu.com/husseinibrahim4/docs/yaser_alwan_book (accessed August 1, 2022). A more comprehensive selection of the work is available on Alwan's personal website (www.yasseralwan.net/) (accessed August 1, 2022).

2   Ibid., p. 102.

3   Yasser Alwan, "Photographing Mohamed Ahmed," in Peacock, ed., *The Liberty of Appearing*, pp. 42–5.

4   Shamoon Zamir, "Egypt Every Day: The Photographs of Yasser Alwan. A Public Conversation," *Electra Street: A Journal of the Arts and Humanities*, issue 1 (Spring 2014), p. 91. Unless otherwise indicated, all comments by Alwan are taken from this conversation and page numbers are given in the text. Where I have used comments drawn from the longer, un-edited and un-revised transcript of the conversation, the comments are marked as "transcript." *Electra Street* is an in-house publication of New York University, Abu Dhabi. The conversation took place on February 8, 2012, on the occasion of a small exhibition of Alwan's photographs at New York University; this exhibition was a continuation of a much larger exhibition held throughout the campus of New York University, Abu Dhabi from October 2012 to April 2013.

5   Zamir, "Egypt Every Day," p. 88.

6   Alwan, "Photographing Mohamed Ahmed," p. 46.

7   Zamir, "Egypt Every Day," p. 88.

8   E-mail to author: June 25, 2018.

9   Judith Butler, *Precarious Life: The Powers of Mourning and Violence* (London: Verso, 2004), p. 20.

10   Judith Butler, *Giving an Account of Oneself* (New York: Fordham University Press, 2005), p. 42.

11   Zamir, "Egypt Every Day," p. 89.

12   Ibid.

13   Ibid., p. 93.

14   Ibid. p. 102.

15   The only example of a context-establishing shot I can think on in Alwan's work is a wide view of the Helwan limestone quarry which he reproduces as a full-page image in *Scream* (p. 47) and a very small image in the margin in *Liberty of Appearing* (p. 12).

16   John Molyneux, introduction to Peacock, ed., *The Liberty of Appearing*, p. 24. Ellipses in the original.

17   Maria Golia, *Cairo: City of Sand* (London: Reaktion Books, 2004), p. 41. Golia uses the spelling *zabbalin* but I have standardized the spelling throughout for the sake of consistency.

18   See Karen Pfeifer, "How Tunisia, Morocco, Jordan, and even Egypt became IMF 'Success Stories' in the 1990s," *Middle East Report*, 210. Reform or Reaction? Dilemmas of Economic Reform in the Middle East (Spring, 1999), pp. 23–7.

19   Eberhard Kienle, "More than a Response to Islamism: The Political Deliberalization of Egypt in the 1990s," *Middle East Journal* 52: 2 (Spring 1998), p. 232.

20   Pfeifer, "IMF 'Success Stories,'" p. 26.

21   Quoted in David Campany, *A Handful of Dust: From the Cosmic to the Domestic* (London: Mack Books, 2017), p. 30.

22   Zamir, "Egypt Every Day," p. 103. The *zabbaleen* have come to international attention in recent years in particular because of two widely seen documentary films: *Marina of the Zabaleen* (Engi Wassaf dir.; Torch Films, 2008), and *Garbage Dreams* (aka *We*

Are the Zabaleen, Mai Iskander, dir., Iskander Film et al, 2009). For typical photographic coverage of the *zabbaleen*, see: "The Zabbaleen of Garbage City" by Peter Dench (http://www.peterdench. com/additional-galleries/the-zabaleen-of-garbage-city/); "In Pictures: Life in Cairo's Garbage City" by Will Carter (http://www.middleeasteye.net/news/ pictures-life-cairo-s-garbage-city-966963438, posted April 14, 2014); "Zabaleen-Cairo" by Marco Bulgarelli (marcobulgarelli.com/zabaleen-cairo/). Dench is a UK-based photographer (see http://www. peterdench.com/biography/); Carter has done a number of photo projects for *Middle East Eye*; while Bulgarelli is an Italian photographer based in Rome (marcobulgarelli.com/biography/). All of the above sites accessed August 11, 2022.

The following books illustrate the academic engagements with Cairo's garbage collectors: Wael Salah Fahmi, *Cairo's Contested Garbage: Sustainable Waste Management System and Zabaleen's Right to the City* (Saarbrücken: Lambert Academic Publishing, 2018); Marie Assaad, *Experiments in Community Development in a Zabbaleen Settlement* (Cairo: American University of Cairo Press, 1994); Elena Volpi and Doaa Abdel Motaal, *The Zabbalin Communirty of Muqattam*, Cairo Papers in Social Science vol. 19, no.4 (Cairo: American University of Cairo, 1999). This last volume contains two studies: Volpi's "Women at the Muqattam Settlement" and Motaal's "Community Organization and Development."

23 Both the quarries and the tanneries have been widely covered by local papers, news agencies, and international news sites. On the quarries, see: "Egyptian Workers Work on a Limestone Quarry," an image portfolio by Ahmed Gomaa, an Egyptian photographer working for the *Associated Press* (http://www.xinhuanet.com/english/ photo/2015-05/30/c_134282673.htm, posted May 30, 2015, no longer available); "Gasping for Air: The Dust-choked World of Egypt's Quarry Workers" by Belal Dardar, an independent Egyptian photographer, inspired to photograph by the Janury 25 Revolution and now in exile from Egypt (http:// www.middleeasteye.net/in-depth/features/dangers-being-quarry-worker-egypt-446420381, posted March 4, 2016); "Deadly White: Into Minya's Quarries" by Mosa'ab Elshamy (http://www.mosaabelshamy. com/deadly-white-egypt) (Elshamy is a young Cairo-based photographer for the *Associated Press*. He switched from a career in pharmacy to photography

following the January 25, 2011, uprisings). "Egyptian Quarrymen" by Amr Abdallah Daish, Cairo-based Egyptian photographer working for the *Reuters* news agency (widerimage.reuters.com/story/egyptian-quarrymen); "Menya's Kids'" by Myriam Abdelaziz, French-American photographer, born in Cairo, and now living and working in New York City (www. myriamabdelaziz.com/menyaskids); "Working in Egypt's Limestone Qyarries – In Pictures" by Khaled Desouki (photographer for AFP-Egypt) (www. theguardian.com/artanddesign/gallery/2020/ feb/27/working-in-egypts-limestone-quarries-in-pictures).

On the tanneries, see: "Leather Tanning: The Harsh Work Behind Egypt's Luxury Products" by Nada Deyaa cultural reporter for Egypt's *Daily News* (dailynewsegypt.com/2016/05/24/leather-tanning-the-harsh-work-behind-egypts-luxury-products/); "Inside Old Cairo's Leather Tanneries" by Abdelrhman Mohamed for *Egypt Today* (www.egypttoday. com/Article/10/3107/Inside-Old-Cairo-s-Leather-Tanneries, posted June 13, 2016); "Tanneries of Old Cairo" by French photographer Magali Courouge (www.madamasr.com/en/2012/10/10/panorama/u/ the-tanneries-of-old-cairo-by-magali-corouge/ posted October 2, 2012). All of the above available sites accessed August 1, 2022.

24 Zamir, "Egypt Every Day," p. 89.

25 See Yasser Alwan, "'The Awakening of a Radical Reality?' Photo Cairo 5," *Jadaliyaa,* February 11, 2013 (www.jadaliyya.com/Details/28023) (last accessed August 2, 2022).

26 Yasser Alwan, "Traces, Fragments, Scraps: Collecting Cairo's Discarded Images," *Jadaliyaa,* June 20, 2017 (www.jadaliyya.com/Details/34345/ Traces,-Fragments,-Scraps-Collecting-Cairo%E2%80%99s-Discarded-Images) (last accessed August 2, 2022).

27 Alwan, "Traces, Fragments, Scraps."

28 All the images I have described can be found as accompaniments to Alwan, "Traces, Fragments, Scraps." Alwan donated his collection of 3,000 images to Akkasah, the photography archive at Al Mawrid, the Arab center for the study of art at New York University, Abu Dhabi.

29 See the recent "Egypt Relaxes Street Photography Ban for Tourists, up to a Point" from Agence France-Presse, *The Guardian*, July 21, 2022 (www.theguardian.com/world/2022/ jul/21/egypt-relaxes-street-photography-ban-for-tourists-up-to-a-point) (last accessed August 2, 2022). The article notes that "the law still forbids pictures of children or those that can 'damage country's image.'" Over a thousand of the images can be seen currently at the *Akkasah* website: akkasah.org/en/results/Yasser%20Alwan%20 Collection?filter=collection_name%3EYasser%20 Alwan%20Collection;;&queries=&pageid=undefined (last accessed August 2, 2022). See also, Shamoon Zamir, "Lost and Found: The Yasser Alwan Collection at Akkasah," *Jadaliyya*, June 19, 2017 (www.jadaliyya. com/Details/34346/Lost-and-Found-The-Yasser-Alwan-Photography-Collection-at-Akkasah) (last accessed August 2, 2022).

30 James R. Mellows, *Walker Evans* (New York: Basic Books, 1997), 213–14. The comments from Evans are from Leslie Katz, "Interview with Walker Evans," *Art in America* (March–April 1971), pp. 82–9.

31 Dorothy Bohm, *Egypt* (London: Thames and Hudson, 1989), with a foreword by Lawrence Durrell and an essay by Ian Jeffrey; Katia Boyadjian and Daniel Juré, *A l'Ombre d'Amon, Carnet d'Egypte* (Paris: Éditions l'Inventaire, Conseil Régional de Basse-Normandie, 2000); Denis Dailleux, *Le Caire* (Paris: Éditions du Chêne, 2006); Carlos Freire and Robert Solé, *Alexandrie l'Egyptienne* (Paris: Éditions Stock, 1998); Sonallah Ibrahim and Jean Pierre Ribière, *Cairo: From Edge to Edge* (Cairo: The American University of Cairo Press, 1998); Olivier Dalle and Frédéric Soreau, *Le Caire/1999* (Lyon: Éditions d'Avers, 1999). All the photographers named, except for Bohm, are either French or based in France: Boyadjian, who is of Armenian origin (and incidentally the niece of the famous Egyptian photographer Van Leo), was born in Cairo. Some of these works are fugitive works in the sense that they are published by relatively small presses or arise out of regional exhibitions—the list of titles here should not, therefore, be taken as being in any way exhaustive.

32 Paul Strand and James Aldridge, *Living Egypt* (An Aperture Book; New York: Horizon Press, 1969).

33 Butler, *Giving an Account of Oneself*, 63–4.

This book was made possible by the support of
Al Mawrid, Arab Center for Art at New York University, Abu Dhabi
and is part of the Center's publication series.

Colophon

Editor: Shamoon Zamir
Managing editor: Ala Younis
Project management: Fabian Reichel
Copyediting: George MacBeth
Graphic design: Rutger Fuchs Amsterdam
Typeface: Akzidenz Grotesk
Production: Thomas Lemaître
Reproductions: DruckConcept, Berlin
Printing: Printer Trento S.R.L.
Paper: Gardamatt Ultra, 150 g/m²

Distributed by
Hatje Cantz Verlag GmbH
Mommsenstraße 27
10629 Berlin
www.hatjecantz.com
A Ganske Publishing Group Company

ISBN 978-3-7757-5370-8

Printed in Italy